NAPLES DECLARED

NAPLES DECLARED

A Walk Around the Bay

BENJAMIN TAYLOR

A MARIAN WOOD BOOK
Published by G. P. Putnam's Sons
a member of Penguin Group (USA) Inc.
New York

A MARIAN WOOD BOOK
Published by G. P. Putnam's Sons
Publishers Since 1838
a member of the Penguin Group
Penguin Group (USA) Inc., 375 Hudson Street, New York, New York 10014, USA •
Penguin Group (Canada), 90 Eglinton Avenue East, Suite 700, Toronto, Ontario M4P 2Y3,
Canada (a division of Pearson Penguin Canada Inc.) • Penguin Books Ltd,
80 Strand, London WC2R 0RL, England • Penguin Ireland, 25 St Stephen's Green,
Dublin 2, Ireland (a division of Penguin Books Ltd) • Penguin Group (Australia),
250 Camberwell Road, Camberwell, Victoria 3124, Australia (a division of Pearson
Australia Group Pty Ltd) • Penguin Books India Pvt Ltd, 11 Community Centre,
Panchsheel Park, New Delhi–110 017, India • Penguin Group (NZ), 67 Apollo Drive,
Rosedale, North Shore 0632, New Zealand (a division of Pearson New Zealand Ltd) •
Penguin Books (South Africa) (Pty) Ltd, 24 Sturdee Avenue, Rosebank,
Johannesburg 2196, South Africa

Penguin Books Ltd, Registered Offices: 80 Strand, London WC2R 0RL, England

Pages 207–210 constitute an extension of this copyright page.

Library of Congress Cataloging-in-Publication Data

Taylor, Benjamin, date.
Naples declared : a walk around the bay / Benjamin Taylor.
p.   cm.
"A Marian Wood book."
Includes bibliographical references and index.
ISBN 978-0-399-15917-6
1. Naples (Italy)—Description and travel.   2. Naples, Bay of (Italy)—Description
and travel.   3. Naples (Italy)—History.   4. Naples, Bay of (Italy)—History.
5. Naples (Italy)—Social life and customs.   6. City and town life—Italy—Naples.
7. Taylor, Benjamin—Travel—Italy—Naples.   I. Title.
DG844.2.T39   2012   2011049450
945'.731—dc23

Printed in the United States of America
1   3   5   7   9   10   8   6   4   2

Book design by Susan Walsh

While the author has made every effort to provide accurate telephone numbers
and Internet addresses at the time of publication, neither the publisher nor the
author assumes any responsibility for errors, or for changes that occur after
publication. Further, the publisher does not have any control over and does not
assume any responsibility for author or third-party websites or their content.

Penguin is committed to publishing works of quality and integrity.
In that spirit, we are proud to offer this book to our readers;
however, the story, the experiences, and the words
are the author's alone.

In memory of the fearless journalist Giancarlo Siani,

born September 19, 1959, in Naples,

graduate of Liceo Ginnasio Statale G. B. Vico and

Università degli Studi di Napoli Federico II,

assassinated by Camorrist cowards in via Vincenzo Romaniello,

Quartiere del Vomero,

September 23, 1985.

We do not know the Hells and Heavens of people we pass in the street. There are two possible perspectives. According to the first, on a minuscule ball of earth, in a smudge of mold called a city, some microorganisms move around, less durable than mayflies. And the internal states of beings, deprived of any reason for their existence, perfectly interchangeable, what importance can they have? According to the second perspective, that of a reversed telescope, every one of these beings grows up to the size of a cathedral, and surpasses in its complexity any nature, living or inert. Only in the second case can we see that no two persons are identical and that we may at best try to guess what is going on inside our fellow men.

—Czesław Miłosz, *Unattainable Earth*

CONTENTS

CHRONOLOGY

Circa 1800–1600 B.C.

Mycenaean traders establish entrepôt at Vivara, island
lying between Ischia and Procida.

Circa 1000–900 B.C.

Greek sailors from Rhodes found Parthenope on what are now
Megaride Island and Pizzofalcone Hill.

Circa 600 B.C.

Cumaean Greeks found Neapolis, or "New City."

474 B.C.

In Bay of Neapolis, Syracusan tyrant Hiero, in alliance with
Aristodemus of Cumae, devastates Etruscan fleet, halting
southward expansion of Etruscans.

Circa 400 B.C.

Samnites conquer Bay.

326 B.C.

Neapolis under Roman domination.

321 B.C.

Samnites humiliate Romans at battle of Caudine Forks.
City under Samnite rule again.

304 B.C.

Neapolis once again Roman.

298–290 B.C.

Samnites confederating with Etruscans, Umbrians, and Gauls are defeated by Rome.

282 B.C.

Final Roman defeat of Etruscans.

90–89 B.C.

Campania region, including Neapolis, granted Roman citizenship, but retains Greek character.

82 B.C.

Rome decimates Samnites, last remaining enemy among Italic peoples.

A.D. 79

Mount Vesuvius erupts, devastating much of area near Neapolis. Pompeii, Herculaneum, Oplontis, Boscoreale, Boscotrecase, Stabiae, and other towns buried in volcanic mud and ash.

476

Last Western Roman emperor, Romulus Augustulus, deposed and imprisoned in Neapolitan villa of Lucullus, later site of Castel dell'Ovo.

536

Byzantine general Belisarius conquers Bay.

553

Naples becomes duchy under Byzantine Empire.

600

Onslaught of Lombards deflected.

763

Under Byzantine bishop Duke Stephen II, Duchy of Naples becomes hereditary and autonomous.

915

Battle of the Garigliano. Saracens finally repulsed after repeated attacks on Naples.

1139

Duchy of Naples conquered by Norman kingdom of Sicily under King Roger II.

Circa 1165

Naples' first castle, Castel Capuano, built as Norman command center.

1194

Henry VI, son-in-law of Roger II, crowned king of Sicily.

1224

University of Naples founded by Holy Roman Emperor Frederick II.

1266

Battle of Benevento. Charles I of Anjou defeats Manfred, son of Frederick II.

1268

Battle of Tagliacozzo. Charles I defeats Conradin (Corradino), grandson of Frederick II. Conradin, last heir to Norman throne, beheaded in piazza Mercato. Charles declares Naples capital of Angevin kingdom.

1279

Construction of Castel Nuovo (later called Maschio Angioino) begins.

1309

Robert of Anjou, called Robert the Wise, crowned king of Naples.

1340

Church and Convent of Santa Chiara completed.

1343

Death of Robert the Wise. Granddaughter Giovanna I succeeds him. Petrarch in residence at Convent of San Lorenzo Maggiore.

1381

Carlo Durazzo usurps throne; reigns as Carlo III. Later has Giovanna I murdered.

1386

Death of Carlo Durazzo. Succeeded by son Ladislao I.

1414

Ladislao I dies, perhaps poisoned. Succeeded by his sister, who reigns as Giovanna II.

1421

Alfonso V of Aragon named heir to Angevin dynasty by Giovanna II.

1435

Death of Giovanna II, followed by struggle between Houses of Anjou and Aragon for Naples.

1442

Alfonso V of Aragon conquers city,
defeating René of Anjou, and begins rule
as Alfonso I of Naples, called the Magnanimous. Constructs Triumphal Arch
between towers of Castel Nuovo to memorialize his victory.

*Triumphal Arch of Alfonso V
of Aragon, Castel Nuovo*

1458

Death of Alfonso the Magnanimous. Succeeded by natural son Ferdinand I, called
Ferrante.

1486

"Barons' Conspiracy," rebellion of southern Italian nobles
allied with Pope Innocent III against Aragonese dominion,
is thwarted.

1494–1495

Death of Ferrante. Son Alfonso II briefly king of Naples. His
death sparks protracted Italian Wars. King Charles VIII of
France claims Naples by right of inheritance from Angevins;
rules for several months.

1499–1504

Great-power war for Kingdom of Naples. Spain prevails.

1504

"El Gran Capitán" Gonzalo Fernández de Córdoba enters
Naples by request of King Ferdinand II of Spain (Ferdinand
the Catholic) and serves as viceroy.

1510

Ramón de Cardona-Anglesola, fourth Spanish viceroy, fails in his attempt to bring Spanish (as opposed to papal) Inquisition to Naples.

1532–1552

Don Pedro de Toledo, eleventh viceroy, promotes expansion and modern town plan for Naples.

1631

Vesuvius erupts.

1637

Neapolitans begin building memorial spire, Guglia di San Gennaro, in gratitude to patron saint for sparing them from eruption.

1647

Fisherman and smuggler Tommaso Aniello d'Amalfi, better known as Masaniello, leads popular rebellion against Spanish-imposed taxation.

1656

Outbreak of plague devastates Naples; one-third of population dies.

1688

Much of city devastated by earthquake.

1697

Philosopher and historian Giambattista Vico named professor of rhetoric at University of Naples.

1707

Short period of Austrian viceroyalty begins.

1719

Church of San Michele Arcangelo on island of Capri
completed.

1725

First edition of Vico's *Principi di una scienza nuova d'intorno
alla comune natura delle nazioni* published.

1734

Naples becomes autonomous kingdom again, under
Charles III of Bourbon.

1738

Initial excavations at Herculaneum.

1759

Charles III abdicates throne in order to be crowned king
of Spain; son Ferdinand IV succeeds him. Prime Minister
Bernardo Tanucci is *de facto* ruler.

1764

William Hamilton posted by King George III as British envoy
plenipotentiary to court of Naples, where he will remain
until 1800.

1768

Ferdinand IV marries Maria Carolina, daughter of Emperor
Francis I and Empress Maria Theresa of Austria. Maria
Carolina rules as queen consort of Naples and Sicily.

1787

Johann Wolfgang von Goethe visits Bay on his journey
through Italy.

1799

Republican revolution succeeds in January, but is overthrown in June; republican leaders not already in exile are executed in piazza Mercato or sentenced to lengthy prison terms. Ferdinand's kingdom is reestablished.

1806

Napoleon Bonaparte, having conquered Kingdom of Naples, names his brother Joseph king.

1808

Joseph Bonaparte, named king of Spain, abdicates Neapolitan throne; Joachim Murat, the Bonapartes' brother-in-law, succeeds him.

1815

Joachim Murat executed after fleeing to Calabria. Ferdinand returns again to Naples, now as king of Two Sicilies.

1820

Ferdinand signs constitution, only to repeal it a year later.

1825

Death of Ferdinand. Son succeeds him as Francis I.

1830

Death of Francis I. Son succeeds him as Ferdinand II.

1837

Giacomo Leopardi dies in Naples, where he has lived for more than three years.

1839

First railway in Italy, Naples–Portici line, opens.

1848

Revolution restores constitution and creates parliament,
but both are dissolved a year later.

1859

Francis II becomes last king of Two Sicilies upon death of his
father, Ferdinand II.

1860

Giuseppe Garibaldi enters Naples; Kingdom of Two Sicilies
annexed to Piedmontese crown under Vittorio Emanuele II;
first united Kingdom of Italy proclaimed in plebiscite.

1880

Vesuvius funicular inaugurated.

1884

More than fourteen thousand die in cholera
epidemic.

1885

Slum areas razed as part of urban renewal
plan that includes construction of Galleria
Umberto I, named for second king of Italy.

Galleria Umberto I, circa 1890

1889–1891

First funicular connects lower town to Chiaia district. First
section of Cuma rail line completed. Circumvesuviana rail line
opens. First funicular connects lower town to Vomero district.

1901

Relationship between government and Camorra revealed in
inquiry headed by Senator Giuseppe Saredo.

1922

Journalist Benito Mussolini and Fascist Blackshirts convene in Naples on October 24, days before March on Rome.

1928–1941

Carità district, notable for its Fascist-era architecture, developed in old San Giuseppe quarter.

1943

Fall of Mussolini in July. Germany declares war on newly established pro-Allied government of Marshal Pietro Badoglio. Neapolitan partisans and street gangs expel German forces from city in "Four Days of Naples." Allied occupation begins.

1944

Vesuvius erupts.

1949

La pelle (*The Skin*) by Curzio Malaparte published; banned by Catholic Church.

1952

After being closed by Fascist authorities in 1938, Caffè Gambrinus reopens.

March 20, 1944

1972

Historic part of Naples protected as cultural heritage by city-planning regulations.

1975

Bypass road opened to relieve traffic congestion at border of old town.

1980

Massive earthquake throughout Campania and Basilicata—
known as Terremoto dell'Irpinia—badly damages Naples and
claims some three thousand lives. Aftermath inspires plan to
revitalize city's outskirts.

1993

First subway line completed.

1994

Naples hosts G7 summit.

2004

In northern periphery, outbreak of war between Di Lauro and
Scissionisti gangs for control of drug trade.

2006

Roberto Saviano publishes *Gomorrah*, unsparing exposé of
full extent of Camorra control of southern Italian economy
and tentacular reach of organized crime into international
business.

2008

Months-long garbage crisis throughout metropolitan Naples.
At Scampia, in northern slums of city, frequent violence
against immigrant Gypsy and African communities.

2011

Renewed garbage crisis. Prime Minister Silvio Berlusconi
orders military to Naples to clear away tens of thousands of
tons of refuse.

DINTORNI DI NAPOLI

1:500.000

0   5   10   20 Chilometri
0 2 4 6 8 10 12 Engl. Miles

———— Tramvie,   ········· Acquedotti

NAPLES DECLARED

One Hundred Fifty Generations

To talk of "entering" the past is absurd. But one can be entered by it, to a degree.

—Elizabeth Bowen, *A Time in Rome*

This takes place years ago: Heeding warnings I've heard about gifted pickpockets, I put my passport in my sock and wade into the teeming streets. My guidebook directs me to the Duomo, where San Gennaro's blood miraculously liquefies twice a year. His relics repose in the dazzling Chapel of the Treasure, encrusted with gold, silver, and precious stones, inlaid with colored marbles—a soaring grotto of the High Baroque, every surface announcing the Church Militant. As it happens, a very satisfactory miracle has taken place the previous morning, and Gennaro's blood is on view again today. The padre turns and turns the crystal reliquary to show that liquefaction has occurred. A hundred schoolchildren line up to press their lips to the glass.

My passport, meanwhile, has ridden up my sock and is now somewhere on the cathedral floor.

Blood of San Gennaro

A couple of hours later, in another part of town, when I realize what has happened, I retrace my steps, legs turning to gravy. Every word of Italian deserts me. (It's a passport, for heaven's sake, easily replaceable at the American consulate. My anguish is an affront to stateless persons everywhere.) When I get back to the cathedral, I find that it has closed for the afternoon. A few mendicant dogs lie about the front steps in a manner specific to southern Italy: on their sides, as if dead. It is a blistering day, and an elderly man sits fanning himself in the shade of the central door—with my passport. He's been *waiting* for me; and I can say with Goethe, on his arrival here, "Either I have always been mad or I am so now." *This* miracle, this superb *gentilezza*, is for real.

Neapolitans call their city Il Cratere—"the big bowl"—and, indeed, its distinctive shape can be only from the impact of a meteor some tens of millions of years ago. As the centuries of conquerors and admirers have observed in their turn, the Bay is an amphitheater open to the sea. Greeks, who came first, more than a millennium before Christ, would have seen it thus. They were from Chalcis, on Euboea—by way of Ischia, where they had established the first Hellenic settlement of any size in the western Mediterranean, and from nearby Cumae, where they had built the first city of Magna Graecia—Greater Greece, as the western expansion has been called from antiquity.

So Naples has always been what it remains, the great open-air theater of Europe. Henry James saw, in 1907, a city "at the best wild and weird and sinister," seated nonetheless "at her ease in her immense natural dignity." What has escaped no traveler is that this oval bay, arms reaching out irregularly into the Tyrrhenian, islands beautifully situated to either side of the mouth of the harbor, makes

Above Mergellina harbor

the loveliest of geologic settings—not least because it is equipped with a reminder of how provisional all loveliness is: Vesuvius, this coast's incomparable emblem of uncertainty, in whose shadow a hundred fifty generations have lived: "Vesuvius, which again and again destroys itself," as Goethe says, "and declares war on any sense of beauty."

Straniero, Neapolitans call everyone not from Naples. Visitors from Milan and London alike are, with a dark quick glance or friendly smile, picked out as *stranieri*. Naples was the last Italian city to develop a middle class—mostly after the Second World War—and its residents know themselves by instinct to be different from other European citizenries: more ancient, less well-off, more skeptical, less clean. But wiser, grander. Two falsifying myths have coexisted. On the one hand, Naples is held to be all superstition, ardor, and mirth; on the other, all cunning, malignity, and deceit. Though distinguished travelers seem to have acquiesced in one stereotype or the other, I do not recognize the city I love in either of these caricatures. Goethe called Naples "this school of light-hearted and happy life." Leopardi, who did his long dying here, called it *"una topaia,"* a rat's nest. But Naples the glorious and Naples the ghastly have always been one place.

The English travel writer Norman Lewis, who served with British intelligence in occupied Naples, and whose diary of those months, *Naples '44*, is a peerless document of the Allied campaign, tells of the harrowing days after the departure of the occupying German force. Before fleeing, they had mined a number of the seafront buildings with delayed-action explosives. The detonations, along with widespread malnutrition and the renewed German air raids, had combined to produce the worst death tolls of any Italian city in the war. Here was Naples at one of the most tragic hours of its vast history. "Apocalyptic scenes," Lewis recorded in his diary, "as people clawed about in the ruins, some of them howling like dogs, in the hopeless attempt to rescue those trapped under the masonry. In Pizzo-Falcone a team of roadsweepers were working by lamplight clearing up what looked like a lake of spilled stew where a crowded shelter had received a direct hit."

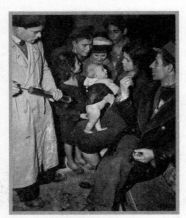

Delousing at air-raid shelter, circa 1943

A captured enemy agent claimed convincingly that thousands of delayed-action mines would be detonated when the city's power supply was restored. A million and a half people were evacuated, all of the lower town. The starving, the injured and sick, the elderly, the new-born, the insane, the about-to-give-birth were herded to the heights of the Vomero, Fontanelle, and the Observatory. Lewis tells of men carrying their parents on their backs, of panic-stricken women and children leaving trails of urine behind them. "At the Vomero," he writes, "we took up positions at a spot on the heights where the road had been intentionally widened to assist visitors to appreci-ate the view, which was splendid indeed. All Naples lay spread out beneath us like an antique map, on which the artist had drawn with almost exaggerated care the many gardens, the castles, the towers and the cupolas. For the first time, awaiting the cataclysm, I appreci-ated the magnificence of this city, seen at a distance which cleansed it of its wartime tegument of grime, and for the first time I realized how un-European, how oriental it was. Nothing moved but a distant floating confetti of doves." The enemy agent turned out to have been lying. Electricity was restored without incident. Neapolitans went back to their desperate wartime lives.

The wonder of the place is that it has not been annihilated by so much history. Ask yourself what New York or Chicago or Los Angeles will be twenty-five centuries from now. Imagination falters. In the course of the terrible seventeenth century alone, Naples suf-fered a volcanic eruption that could well have buried everyone had the cloud of ash settled differently, a plague that did claim one-third of the inhabitants, and an earthquake that reduced much of the city to rubble. These were but the enormities of nature.

Those of man accomplished their considerable work as well. Naples, it has been said, did not perish like Troy or Nineveh or Pompeii. It is, instead, a Pompeii that escaped burial, a living Pom-peii. Therefore it is well, when you walk its streets and *vicoli*, chaotic with life, to save a thought for Pompeii; as, when you stroll the void avenues of Pompeii, to think of Naples.

"Tis generally allowed that Naples is the pleasantest place in Europe," writes Thomas Nugent in the mid–eighteenth century. English milords of the Age of Reason traveled to Europe with *The Grand Tour: Containing an Exact Description of Most of the Cities, Towns, and Remarkable Places of Europe . . . by Mr. Nugent*, four volumes long, in their baggage. The Grand Tour, unlike our tours, could last for many months, even for years. Meant to put the finishing touch on young Englishmen of rank, it culminated at Naples, from which one began the journey home. Grand Tourists ran the gamut; among them were poets, painters, musicians, scholars, collectors, dilettantes, idlers, satyrs, dope fiends, and spies. The Tour had taken shape in Elizabethan times, Philip Sidney being among the first to make it. Inigo Jones made the Tour. So, in their turn, did John Milton, John Evelyn, Joseph Addison, Horace Walpole, Tobias Smollett, Oliver Goldsmith, Edward Gibbon, James Boswell, William Beckford, Lord Byron, and Thomas Macaulay, to mention only the most notable.

With the rise of the steamship and the railroad, the once-and-for-all trip to Europe gave way to repeated journeys. Middle-class tourism as we know it replaced the Grand Tour. A late Victorian guidebook to Naples advises visitors to pay no attention to touters at the railway station; to look sharply after their personal luggage and get as quickly as possible into the omnibus carriage of the hotel they've selected or, if taking a private coach, to beware of any would-be cicerone mounting the box, for he will be entitled to an emolument; finally, if the stomach is empty, to take a medicinal nip of brandy upon inhaling a bad odor. A four-day itinerary of the sights is declared sufficient.

All this edginess and haste resemble the meaner world of our common days, the way we travel now. The Grand Tour resembles a dream. I came to Naples some years ago armed with a few shibboleths and a riddling sentence from the works of Walter Benjamin: "The traveling citizen who gropes his way as far as Rome from one work of art to the next, as along a stockade, loses his nerve in Naples." I loved, to begin with, that phrase "traveling citizen," which seemed a finer thing to be than a tourist. But I could only speculate as to what it meant. A citizen of the republic of those most at home when in strange places, I decided, and felt immediately in the best company. Rule number one of this citizenship is, There are things you will never understand. Everybody acknowledges the breed of bad travel writer who bores you with tales of lost luggage (or lost passports), chiseling cabdrivers, know-nothing concierges, despotic waiters, tainted meals. But such are not the worst. The hottest circle of travel-writing Hell is reserved for know-it-alls who, like Simone de Beauvoir, Jean Baudrillard, or Bernard-Henri Lévy, chatter away without a trace of perplexity. To read these on the United States is to learn how not to write. Their confident abstractions apply only to an abstract America that they knew upon arrival.

Better by far to confess that you're bewildered. I hear an unfamiliar word in the street, shouted after a woman disappearing into the throng of Spaccanapoli—literally, "splits Naples"—the long straight street running down the middle of the ancient center. Noting the chagrin it produces, I pocket *"Zoccola!"*—an epithet with power, it is clear. Later I learn that it is slang for the yellow-toothed, ginger-colored rats that scamper in and out of the boulders down at the harbor. These are *zoccoli*, a word which, in the feminine, also means "whores." In Naples, it is said that the last humiliation for a tomcat is to make love all night to a brand-new sweetheart, only to realize at sunup that she's *una zoccola*. I feel I've entered a realm where no Grand Tour or Cook's Tour could have brought me. But every such revelation of "the real Naples" prompts also the question, How many of the others am I missing? About nine-tenths, I expect.

One spring afternoon, during the long siesta, I go down to the waterfront adjacent to Castel dell'Ovo. Ten or fifteen teenage boys are sunning themselves on the boulders (the very boulders in and out of which *zoccoli* are said to scamper, and this worries me). The youths, each perfect of his kind, are in various states of undress. One decides to put on a show. He takes off his belt and pulls it quickly back and forth against his crotch. Then he puts the belt to his nose and throws back his head in mock ecstasy. Never have I beheld such wanton innocence, and it's something at last that I am confident of understanding. By and large, however, Naples has been a school of bewilderment in which I lose the nerve brought with me from Venice, Florence, and Rome.

Pascal says that our misfortunes spring from not being able to sit quietly in one room. In her poem "Questions of Travel," Elizabeth Bishop rebukes him by listing the sights she would not have been willing to miss. Each of us has such a list. Near the top of mine is the Neapolitan church of Santa Chiara, restored after the war to its original fourteenth-century Gothic severity. It had been Baroqued up; old photographs show "rather a ball-room than a church," as the Victorian travel writer Augustus Hare noted. The Angevin tombs, matchless of their kind and among the great treasures of Italy, cannot have been easy to see amid such splendor. As for the fragmentary frescoes of Giotto and his Neapolitan *scuola*, they'd been plastered over since 1730. (Yet more evidence, if one needed it, of how inexplicable is the history of taste.) The campanile, rebuilt in the fifteenth century, is still hung with the bells that Sancha of Mallorca, unloved second queen of Robert the Wise, donated upon the original consecration in 1340. They make the finest noise in Naples.

Damaged tomb of Robert the Wise,
Santa Chiara

On August 4, 1943, stray incendiaries from Allied planes fell on Santa Chiara. The fire lasted for two days. When it was over, the church was a ruin, all of its masterworks damaged or destroyed. King Robert's tomb had stood some forty feet high before the bombing. Double columns supporting the many-tiered structure had niches for statues of the virtues and saints. The canopy with its bas-relief of the Resurrection is gone now. The effigies of the king in glory and, below, barefoot and wrapped in Franciscan habit on his bier remain, as do the five mourning figures who surround him, but one of two angels who drew back the arras is gone and the other damaged. This battered torso can only intimate what the monument was. Worse for wear but still here, it commands a reverence different from before. Of the Giottos, there are only fragments left to see in the choir of the Poor Clares. You must sneak in for a glance and be quick about it. The sisters, fearsome in their homespun, will drive you out.

I go to dinner with my new friend Paolo, an intern at a hospital in one of the working-class districts of Naples. Paolo is from the North, an impressive man, passionate about doctoring, committed to the care of the poor, and rigorously, harshly intellectual. He's got a fine set of dimples, which he underutilizes. We meet at a café in piazza Bellini, a pretty square in which there are excavations of the ancient Greek walls. Once we've settled in at one of the outdoor tables, I am comfortable enough to ask a touristic question. What is the *malocchio*, the evil eye? I know only this: Hereabouts, according to folk tradition, a look can blight or kill. The previous evening, in piazza Mercato, I got into a loud sneezing fit—traditionally frowned upon in Naples, for sneezing had been considered an early symptom of cholera—and afterward I distinctly thought I felt the evil eye on the back of my neck.

"Is *jettatura* a synonym for the evil eye?" I ask. "And what are *jettatori*?"

"*Jettatura* is the practice of the *malocchio*, the gift for inflicting it. *Jettatori* are persons thus endowed." He looks away, and I can see that his jaw is working. "You find it *colorful*, don't you?" he snaps. "Such atavistic garbage is what has held back the South. Croce said that the most fearsome thing about the *malocchio* is that it doesn't exist. He's a bourgeois thinker, Croce, but this was a brilliant remark, by which he meant that it frightened him to see people in the grip of such nonsense. It frightens me."

Paolo's family is of the highest Communist pedigree. He tells me that his grandfather, in youth a friend of Antonio Gramsci, had been exiled to Abruzzo under the Fascists. An uncle who fought heroically with the Communist armed resistance was captured and killed by Germans. "You know that Communists were *in the majority* here in 1948. You know that we were *defrauded*." Though Paolo was born in the 1960s, when he speaks about the election of

1948 you'd think it was his own heart that broke that year. "Your CIA manipulated the outcome. They enabled the Christian Democrats to steal the election."

"If the Communists had won," I say cautiously, "there might have been no more elections for forty years. Better contested elections with hanky-panky, I say, than a single slate of Soviet-sponsored candidates." I am wiping my feet on his heroic family and their traditions. I do not think this dinner is going to be a success.

"Sinatra was in on it," he tells me. "Frank Sinatra, propagandizing on the Voice of America. Then came black-bag funds from the CIA to all anti-Communist factions." He asks why I am not a Communist, as if asking why I am not a friend to humanity. I explain certain differences between the Italian Communist Party and the CPUSA—that the latter wasn't so much a political party as an espionage operation masquerading as a political party, that the whole setup was funded by Moscow and had everything to do with international power politics and nothing to do with workers of the world, whatever the idealistic membership imagined their party to stand for.

He doesn't follow, or isn't listening. "Who were the heroes of American Communism?" he wants to know. "Who were the martyrs? The Togliattis, the Gramscis?"

"Hiss and Rosenberg were the heroes and martyrs," I say. His gaze brightens at the mention of these names. (If there *were* such a thing as the evil eye, I'd hit him with it now.) Thus dinner limps to its conclusion. I maneuver us to the safe topic of Vesuvius, and ask another of my touristic questions: When did it lose its plume of smoke? Were he to tell me that it had gone dormant to protest irregularities in the '48 elections, I wouldn't be altogether surprised.

The volcano has traditionally been regarded as a commentator on the human scene. When it erupted in the last year of the Second World War, even rationalistic northerners suspected Vesuvius of uttering an opinion.

"The plume disappeared one day after the war. Old people here tell you about it." But vulcanologists, he says, tell you that the dormancy belies a cataclysmic potential. Three millennia from now, or tomorrow morning, Naples will be consumed. At last, Paolo shows his dimples. We say good night with a hesitant *abbraccio*. All the pleasant way home, I savor *"millenni da ora, oppure domani mattina"*—"millennia from now, or tomorrow morning"—his fine phrase.

At Naples, the paganism is perennial: the Greekness, I mean—that underworld, literal and figurative, underpinning the Catholicism practiced here. Consider Venice and Rome, by contrast. In Venice, there is no antiquity at all. In Rome, no Archaic Greek presence. But Naples is a civilization founded by Hellenes, and Greekness has been, despite chances and changes, the living subterranean truth of the place. Originally, Naples was called Parthenope, for the Siren who flung herself into the gulf and washed ashore after Odysseus rejected her. Renamed Neapolis, "New City," by the second wave of Greek colonists—Chalcidians, Athenians, nearby Cumaeans and Ischians—the city established itself as the major western Mediterranean port. At the salient of Pizzofalcone stood a temple to Aphrodite Euploia, granter of prosperous voyages. All this when Rome had yet to emerge from myth into history. At a time when trading ships plied the Gulf of Naples and ambassadors came and went, a she-wolf suckled Romulus and Remus beside the Tiber.

Greece gave the Romans their gods, their arts, their sciences, their fundamental sentiment of life; Roman culture is Greco-Roman. What was most essential to Roman poets and historians was their Greek patrimony: the vitalistic pessimism, in a word, the gift for facing without false hope the conditions of our humanity. After 326 B.C., when it was defeated by Rome militarily, Naples proceeded to conquer Rome culturally. "Conquered Greece conquered its barbaric conqueror," says Horace, "and brought the arts to Rome," referring to the sack of Corinth nearly two centuries later. But the process of Hellenization starts with Rome's fourth-century-B.C. conquest of this bay.

At Naples, from which it spread to Rome, the Greek response to life—natural, canny, sensate, disabused—persists in subtle and overt ways, despite the centuries of permutation. There is, in Naples, a living interdependence between Christian and pagan emotions. It is said that the land is Christian but the water pagan. On land, the Mother of God has her dominion; but Sirens rule the Bay. How shore and sea have coexisted, the triumphant Catholic piety and the submerged Greco-Roman ethos, is perhaps a secret known only to Parthenopeans, but I will try to grasp some part of it in what follows.

Here, says Goethe, one is tossed about between the acts of nature and the acts of humankind. Amalgamated from Greek, Samnite, Roman, Byzantine, Norman, Swabian, Angevin, Aragonese, Spanish, Austrian, Bourbon, Napoleonic, Savoyard, and American elements, along with a dash of Barbary corsair, Neapolitan civilization has been Europe's most extraordinary hybrid. The history of conquest, the long wanting of Naples, is a story that dates at least from the Roman siege and conquest. The Bay has seen armies come and go ever since. Over the course of twenty-four centuries, the changes wrought by successive dominations have made this contested ground what it is—architecturally, artistically, musically, philosophically, spiritually. " 'That red curve of houses follows the wall of the theatre where Nero sang,' " writes Shirley Hazzard in *The Bay of Noon*, her Neapolitan novel: "The big thing below the cathedral had been a paleo-Christian temple. Those columns came from a temple of the Dioscuri, that church was the site of the Roman basilica. The question 'What is it?' took on, here, an aspect of impertinence; one might only learn what it had successively been."

Add to these successive blows of history those of nature and you begin to grasp the strong sense of election that Neapolitans favor, a conviction that they've been the Christ among Italian cities, singled out for harsher testings. At the Convent of San Lorenzo Maggiore, in the autumn of 1343, Petrarch prayed all night for salvation from a storm that seemed to Naples not a turn in the weather but the end of the world. "We found courage in despair," he wrote, "as men do; we mounted our horses and went down to the harbor, to behold and die. . . . The whole shore was strewn with bodies, crushed and still breathing. . . . Amidst all this there was such shouting of men, such shrieking of women, as to drown the noise of the sea and sky. . . . A thousand mountainous waves were coursing between Capri and Naples; the bay was not of an azure hue or black as it generally is in great storms—but hoary with the brightness of the foam." Petrarch, who later fell out of love with Naples, seems never to have cherished it more than at this apocalyptic-seeming moment. Let his words stand here at the outset for other accounts of other calamities.

With the fall of the Bourbon dynasty in 1860, Naples commenced its twilight. A ghastly cholera epidemic in 1884 definitively discouraged northern Europeans from coming. Briefly, nervously, they would pass through en route to Pompeii or Paestum, but the moldering marvels of what had been the second city of continental Europe went increasingly unseen. Thus it remains to this day: not for all tastes. Called the most beautiful of cities in Greco-Roman antiquity, in the High Middle Ages, and again in the eighteenth century, Naples will never again exercise its old allure. Venice must have ten thousand sightseers for every independent soul who seeks out the inner secrets of this place. It is Capri, Ischia, Sorrento, Positano that are the shining destinations. Naples hides its glamour from the hordes on their way to such watering places. "To travelers who offer the insult of a few hours of their time, the city returns its own harsh indifference," Miss Hazzard writes, "plunging them into misadventures and dismissing them." Here is a metropolis that has not become a boutique of itself—for painful reasons, it must be said: underemployment, bureaucracies of legendary ineptitude, widespread exactions by the criminal rackets (the ubiquitous and damnable Camorra). If you wish to leave behind these problems, for they'll be there when you come back, go to the Parco della Tomba di Virgilio on the high cliff above Mergellina harbor. We are no longer permitted to believe that the columbarium at the head of the steep stair is Virgil's tomb. No, it is that of some other Roman, impossible to name. The poet Silius Italicus purchased the hillside in the first century, restored the sepulchre, and celebrated perpetual obsequies for the greatest of Roman bards. The place

Apocryphal tomb of Virgil

has been sacred to poets ever since. A green bay tree that grew nearby is alleged to have withered on the death of Dante. It is said that King Robert the Wise brought Petrarch to plant another (which met a different fate, carried off root and branch by eighteenth-century relic hunters). It is said that here Boccaccio renounced getting and spending and vowed himself to his art. On my most recent visit, I surprised a pair of lovers behind the columbarium. The man bared his teeth. His lady hid her face. I made a quick retreat.

The Parco della Tomba di Virgilio closes each day at half past one in the afternoon. You cannot be there at sunset, as Goethe was, when he saw the last rays shine deeply into the mouth of the adjacent grotto. In any case, you wouldn't see that today, since the tunnel caved in about ninety years ago. Medieval tradition held that Virgil had cut it through the cliff by magic. In reality, it was engineered in the first century B.C. to connect Neapolis to Puteoli (Pozzuoli).

What you will not be wrong to put your trust in is the nearby grave of Leopardi, greatest of Italian poets after Dante. He really does lie there, and how he comes to lie there is a story. Peripatetic in life, he moved around quite a bit after death too. Leopardi probably died in the usual hunchback way, the weight of the deformity finally stopping his heart. It was late spring, 1837. Cholera was raging at the time. The poet was mistaken for a victim of the disease and his body ordered to the lime pit. Only prompt intervention by his friend Antonio Ranieri saved him from a common grave. Leopardi was interred beneath the Church of San Vitale Fuorigrotta. Seven years later, because of the dampness of the crypt, he was brought upstairs. Ranieri spent two hours alone before the open casket. The remains were then placed in the sacristy and a memorial stone put over them. In 1900 the body was moved yet again, this time to a newly constructed porch of San Vitale. In 1939, Leopardi was relocated—one last time, presumably—to the cliff above Mergellina, where in life he had so often come, like poets before him, to contemplate the supposed tomb of Virgil. The grandiose monument

erected at the Parco della Tomba di Virgilio to honor Leopardi is in the best Mussolinian taste. But one recalls that when in Rome, the poet shrugged off pompous mausoleums, saving his reverence for the very modest resting place of Torquato Tasso in the Church of Sant'Onofrio—"ashes marked by nothing but a bare stone, a span-and-a-half in length and breadth, hidden away in the corner of a poor little church ... This poverty suffices to interest and inspire posterity." He

Death mask of Giacomo Leopardi

seems most worth revering, Leopardi, who above all other Neapolitans, native or naturalized or honorary, knew the art of what and how to revere.

In his long poem "La ginestra o il fiore del deserto" ("Broom" in English), written at Torre del Greco, a town at the foot of Vesuvius brightened each spring by the low-growing broom in flower, as everywhere on the slopes of the volcano, Leopardi speaks of "Sterminator Vesevo," Vesuvius the Exterminator, and of the hardy vines blossoming there in defiance. These are the poles of his great poetry: the horrifying mountain and the yellow flower in bloom. At the conclusion of his *Canti* (a book that is to Italians what *Les fleurs du mal* is to French readers or *Leaves of Grass* to American), knowing that annihilating nature, epitomized in the volcano, must prevail, Leopardi offers this advice:

> *You, about to take*
> *the fatal step*
> *that leads to Pluto's kingdom,*
> *commit to present pleasure*
> *your brief life.*

I have. I will.

You are a traveling citizen if you entertain the possibility that what you think you are seeing is not what you are seeing; that unauthorized emotions are preferable to authorized; and that when you arrive at a formula you are most likely lost. Harold Acton, traveling citizen *par excellence* and nuanced lover of Naples, tells the following story in *The Bourbons of Naples*: In the happy splendor of their early reign, before everything went so terribly wrong, King Ferdinand I and Queen Maria Carolina favored an aristocratic convent of the old city with a royal visit. One tended to eat and drink well at such wealthy convents; the royal palates hadn't been disappointed. But their Bourbon majesties were puzzled when the abbess showed them to another dining room, where a sideboard groaned with roasted fowl and various fish. Lunch after lunch, it appeared. Then the sisters began to carve and slice what were in fact ices and *gelati* in the shapes of fowl and fish. I like to think of these whimsical, perhaps wise nuns perpetrating such pleasure. Our life sentence is not to know what comes next. But if doomed to the terrors of the unexpected, we are reprieved by the delights of it, large and small: every epicurean's argument. On the evening of my most recent return—Vesuvius clear of clouds, the lanterns of a few fishing boats flickering in the harbor, some scraps of song floating up from Mergellina, and Capri's lights dimly visible at the vanishing point—a full moon rose over the world's most famous bay. I looked awhile, went for a drink, looked again. A bite had been taken from the lower left-hand quadrant of the moon. I got comfortable at my window and watched the whole eclipse, then dreamed Naples had arranged it (such hospitality, they shouldn't have) to welcome me back. In this place, my dream said, trust to the promise of renewable wonder, every lover's hope and prayer.

ONE

From Pithekoussai

... Their dining
Puts us to shame: we can only envy a people
  So frugal by nature it costs them

No effort not to guzzle and swill. Yet (if I
  Read their faces rightly after ten years)
They are without hope. The Greeks used to call the Sun
  He-who-smites-from-afar, and from here, where

Shadows are dagger-edged, the daily ocean blue,
  I can see what they meant: his unwinking
Outrageous eye laughs to scorn any notion
  Of change or escape, and a silent

Ex-volcano, without a stream or a bird,
  Echoes that laugh.

—W. H. Auden, "Good-Bye to the Mezzogiorno"

*O*n a morning ferry, the roadstead to Ischia takes me past villas along the Posillipo coast, some spiffy, some woebegone. Palazzo degli Spiriti, a Roman ruin visible only from the sea, seems a death's-head staring back. Beyond the headland, to starboard, there's a sudden view of Campi Flegrei and, off the port side,

Ruins of Palazzo degli Spiriti

Procida, the site for a century and a half of a large prison. It remains no more than a penitential rock in the minds of many; but those who've read *Arturo's Island*, Elsa Morante's lyrical novel, imagine Procida quite differently. The heightened splendors and miseries of the little hero's childhood, played out as if according to a timeless law precluding all thought of what, elsewhere, history has contrived, incline you to mythical surmises. Arturo says: "The present seemed to me eternal, like a magic feast." His island has certainly been magic for me till today. I vividly remember reading the book at my father's bedside in the weeks after an operation on his heart. Mother and I would spell each other. We were in Cleveland, where the doctors had a particularly high rate of success with the tricky procedure. It had been snowing for days, and when sun-drenched Arturo licked the salt off himself, or wrote in the sand "ARTURO GERACE IS ALONE, ALWAYS ALONE," or just for practice kissed his boat or an orange he was eating or a cat in the road, I felt translated to a milieu where nothing unmanageably bad could happen and loneliness was bliss.

It emerges that Arturo's father is in the grip of some mania. Hollow-eyed and half absent, he drags himself around the island. Arturo follows him one day to a hill beneath the prison walls, and watches as his father, head thrown back, howls a Neapolitan love song. Then, switching to another tack, he begins to whistle in a code of longs and shorts that Arturo, mad with jealousy, recog-

nizes as the private Morse that
father and son have developed for
use between themselves. Arturo's
father has obviously taught it to
someone else. He whistles to the
castle walls: "NO—VISITS—NO—
LETTERS—NOTHING.
AT—LEAST—ONE—WORD.
WHAT—WOULD—IT—COST—
YOU?" And Arturo can readily
grasp the curtly whistled answer that

Afternoon in Procida

comes from the barred window—*"VATTENE, PARODIA!"*—not altogether easy to put into English, but "GET LOST, YOU FREAK
SHOW!" approximates. Evidently Arturo's father comes round
every day, seeking this same mortification beneath the barred window of a handsome young criminal with whom he's fallen in love.

My own father lay restless in his hospital bed, looking at us with
childlike eyes, frightened by the breathing tube. Secrets aplenty
he had, but I'm doubtful that among them was anything along the
lines of Arturo's father's. Dad recovered. Mom took him home to
their life. I went back to mine.

Procida is a piece of Ischia torn free by a prehistoric
earthquake. Strabo and Pliny the Elder already knew this (as they
would also have recognized that Capri was once a piece of the Sorrentine Peninsula). The islet of Vivara is similarly an erstwhile piece
of Procida, linked now by a bridge, and here confounding archaeological finds have been made, revealing the presence of Greeks a

thousand years earlier than had been thought. In the Middle Bronze Age—that is, seventeen or eighteen centuries before Christ— vigorous maritime contact between the Aegean and the Tyrrhenian had been established; for a millennium before the founding of the first Greek cities on the mainland and in Sicily, Greeks traveled these waters.

Imagine whole ages of man, rather than forty-some-odd years, intervening between Lewis and Clark and the settling of the American West. These Greeks were Mycenaeans, most of whose cities collapsed in the thirteenth century B.C. What followed was a Dark Age, and it was another four centuries before the Archaic Greek culture of Homeric poetry and western settlement emerged, the Greece that built Cumae and Parthenope and Neapolis.

As one moves back in historic time, the scale changes. A hundred years of the Bronze Age are like ten of our own. In the reckoning of prehistoric time—Neolithic, Mesolithic, Upper Paleolithic—the scale changes dizzyingly. One's notion of the Bronze Age world of 1800 B.C., to be comprehensible, should perhaps be set against a few human-making milestones. Our genus, *Homo*, fashioned tools about 2.8 million years ago. *Homo erectus* (also called *Homo ergaster*) made his way out of Africa and into Europe and Asia about 800,000 years after that, and mastered fire 400,000 years ago, and began burying the dead 80,000 years ago. Only about 35,000 years ago did our species, *Homo sapiens*, the ultimately successful hominid, begin creating the images and objects now called art. About 24,000 years after that we learned the secret of making wheat germinate in the earth, and of harnessing animals to plow it. About 5,000 years after that, the first cities were built, in Mesopotamia and Egypt. A millennium or so after that, probably in present-day

Iran, we smelted copper, precursor to the all-important bronze that would come of admixing tin and give the age its name. Such prehistoric dates are heuristic; a stunning new find may upend one or another of them. But I like impositions of order, I like the illusion of clarity. Therefore let us say that one fine morning, about 7,000 years after the invention of agriculture and 2,000 after the beginnings of urban life, Mycenaean Greeks sailed through the Strait of Messina and beheld the western shores of Italy.

We know these Achaeans, as they called themselves, because Homer sang their fames—the glory of iron-hearted Achilles, the homecoming of many-minded Odysseus—in the eighth century B.C., as had a long tradition of oral poets (*aoidoi*) preceding him. Why these Mycenaeans vanished, nobody can say, but archaeologists have established that around 1230 B.C. their palaces were pulled down and their cities abandoned.

We know, by contrast, that their precursors the Minoans, based in Crete, having survived Indo-European invasions in the twenty-fourth century B.C. and after, succumbed in the end to a volcanic eruption at Thera (modern-day Santorini) in about 1620 B.C., a cataclysm that produced earthquakes, tidal waves, darkness throughout the eastern Mediterranean and a vast, life-destroying fallout of ash—among the greatest natural disasters in human history. But the fate of the Mycenaeans, the civilization that supplanted and subsumed the Minoans, is far less explicable. It was formerly believed that the palaces at Athens, Mycenae, Corinth, Pylos, Tiryns, and other Greek cities were laid waste by Dorian invaders wielding iron weapons. Archaeology now shows them to have arrived at least a hundred years after the destruction of those palaces, and wielding not iron but bronze. And why, anyhow, would invaders have destroyed palaces but left cities standing? No, the Achaeans were not annihilated by Dorian invaders. A clue to what actually happened may be in the excavations at Mycenae itself, as the granary of the palace was the first structure to be destroyed. Did famine drive the populations of that city and others to attack those who held power and hoarded food? What happened to the Mycenaeans may not be too different from what probably happened to the Anasazi of the North American Southwest in the thirteenth century: Rain got too scarce; life got too hard; and cities, perhaps on the advice of a god, were abandoned for someplace more promising.

Whatever did happen, the Mycenaean Greeks strewed their handiwork throughout the Mediterranean before vanishing. In the Museo Archeologico Regionale of Agrigento, in Sicily, is a marvelously preserved little three-handled unguent jar, fashioned and painted as only Achaean craftsmen could, and datable to the fifteenth century B.C. In what sailing ships did such things make their way to Sicilian and Tyrrhenian coasts and beyond? We have knowledge of the animal-hide vessels that plied the Tigris and Euphrates from later Paleolithic times, and of the reed boats that superseded them, and of square-rigged boats on the Nile from the fourth millennium B.C. But about the earliest *seamanship* we know next to nothing. Phoenician rafts made for hugging the shore may well have ventured into open waters as long ago as the eighth, ninth, or tenth millennium B.C., in which case seamanship would not be much younger than river navigation. Many-oared vessels with prows and keels are attested in the Aegean by the fourth millennium B.C., and sailing ships in the Tyrrhenian by perhaps the start of the second.

Consider the courage of those most ancient mariners. Anyone

who's spent time on the mercurial Mediterranean will readily imagine the short work a squall could make of knocked-together Phoenician or Greek craft. Not until the rib-hulled ship and use of bitumen for caulking did men stand a better-than-even chance of coming through heavy weather. These innovations came to Europe around the eighth century B.C. Only then did Greeks, post–Dark Age Greeks, that is, Archaic Greeks, successors to the Bronze Age Mycenaeans they would forever mythologize in song as their heroes and half-gods, begin founding cities in the "Far West," where Odysseus, the man of many turns, had wandered on his circuitous way home. The most authoritative geographical information early navigators had about Evening Lands must have been based on the bardic traditions culminating in Homer. The west was exorbitance and strong poetry, and westwardness the great romantic draw, the mystery at the edge of the map, as it would be again and again in European history. Homer's *Odyssey* reflects the mythmaking of an age of exploration as surely as Montaigne's "On Cannibals" or Shakespeare's *Tempest*. Calypso's island; the lands of the Cyclops, the Laestrygonians, the Phaeacians; the song of the Sirens; the twin threats of Scylla and Charybdis; the Isle of the Dead—these were wonders and enormities marking out the limits of the world. Are such tall tales not the imaginative by-product of any westward push, whether across the Atlantic to the New World in the sixteenth century or ever deeper into North and South America in the seventeenth, eighteenth, and nineteenth?

As every American schoolchild used to know, President Jefferson dispatched Meriwether Lewis, William Clark, and their thirty-some-man Corps of Discovery to see what lay west and, more practically, to find that will-o'-the-wisp the Northwest Passage to the

Orient. Were I to speculate as to what kind of very ancient Greek made his way to the Tyrrhenian Sea, I'd take as my reference point Lewis and Clark's ill-assorted Corps: young men with little to lose and kingdoms to win.

The Greeks who came this way, eight centuries before Christ, had learned from Phoenicians a way of telling true north not by the Charioteer and the Great Bear but by the Little Bear instead. This enabled them in fair weather to navigate all night, says Strabo. The earliest Phoenician and Achaean mariners must have kept to the Greek coast and islands as far as Corcyra, present-day Corfu, then come across the Strait of Otranto, then hugged the bottom of the boot to the Strait of Messina. But a much quicker way west, and quicker still by all-night sailing, was boldly through the middle of the sea. Greek settlers made their way west along a chain of stopping-off places from Crete to the Balearics. In about 600 B.C. they founded Massalia, modern-day Marseille. (Simultaneously, they were establishing cities around the rim of the Black Sea and, more sparsely, along the Adriatic. At the mouth of the River Reno, south of the Po Delta, is one of the world's wonders, though unvisitable because submerged: Spina, an ancient Greek Venice, canals and grid plan visible from the air.) And if they never made a Greek lake of the Mediterranean—Phoenicians and Carthaginians were as present and as enterprising—theirs was the culture that lived on to shape the subsequent centuries. Fernand Braudel, preeminent historian of the Mediterranean, says: "Like the souls of the dead who were brought to life by Odysseus' sacrifices, Greek thought is constantly being reincarnated, transmitted to us. It was to be found in Miletus in the great days of the Ionians; in Athens when Socrates was teaching there; in Alexandria in Egypt, before the brilliant age of Archimedes in Syracuse; it was still alive in Rome, since the pathetic reduction of Greece to a Roman province in 146 B.C. was in the end a spiritual triumph by the conquered over the conquerors; it was a precious bloom cherished in a hothouse by Byzantium, that second Rome; it flowered once more in the Florence of Lorenzo de' Medici and Pico della Mirandola. . . ." Phoenicia and Carthage are dead and gone; but Greece is a self-renewing resource, with us always.

Pithekoussai, Island of Monkeys, was the name that settlers from the Aegean cities of Chalcis and Eretria, on Euboea, gave to the outpost they established here on the Bay—on what we know as Ischia—perhaps because they regarded it as wild and remote enough for monkeys, though there certainly never were any. Having come so far, these Archaic sailors and merchants believed they might be near the mythical river encircling earth and dividing it from Hades. In the shadow of Monte Epomeo they built an Archaic equivalent to the early settlements of our own American Wild West.

Within a century, Epomeo, which turned out to be an extremely destructive volcano, annihilated the settlement. (This is the "ex-volcano" Auden refers to in "Good-Bye to the Mezzogiorno.") Having erupted for the last time in the Middle Ages, it has been ever since a pleasant hill to climb in spring or fall. On this February morning, there's a dusting of snow at the summit—for the first time in a decade, people tell me.

Ischia in the off-season is run by drunkards and cats. In summer, the tourists in their hundreds of thousands, Germans especially, come for the curative waters, "the boiling springs," as Auden calls them in "Ischia,"

which betray her secret fever,
    make limber the gout-stiffened joint

and improve the venereal act; your ambient peace
in any case is a cure for, ceasing to think
        of a way to get on, we
    learn to simply wander about

by twisting paths which at any moment reveal
some vista as an absolute goal; eastward, perhaps,
        suddenly there, Vesuvius,
    looming across the bright bland bay

like a massive family pudding, or, around
a southern point, sheer-sided Capri who by herself
        defends the cult of Pleasure,
    a jealous, sometimes a cruel, god.

*W. H. Auden at Mary's International Bar
and Café, Ischia, with proprietress
Maria Senese, 1950*

However, I'm not one for taking the waters, and I share Norman Douglas's laughing contempt: "Does the hair of your eyelashes drop out? Try Bagno di Piaggia Romana.... Headache, chill on the liver, or kidney trouble? Bagno di Fontana. Does your nose itch? The Sudatorio di Castiglione. Tooth-ache or impetigo? Bagno di Succellaro ... Does your grandfather complain of baldness, are you troubled with elephantiasis, or is your wife anxious to be blessed with children? Hasten, all three of you, to the Bagno di Citara." Such nonsense was the modern making of the island. But I like my Ischia shuttered and mournful, with scarcely a shop or restaurant or curative spring to beckon you. (It puts me in mind of Martha's Vineyard in winter, as Capri in winter puts me in mind of Nantucket.) Auden and Chester Kallman, the great poet's wastrel boyfriend, braved the throng for summers on end, about twelve in all, and might have continued but for a nasty bit of business. Their caretaker and houseboy, one Giocondo, routinely got 60,000 lire for off-season maintenance of the house at Forio, the Ischian town where Auden and Kallman lived. One winter, in a fit of absent-mindedness, Auden wrote the check for 600,000. Giocondo cashed it and, when challenged, announced all over the island that he'd earned that money the hard way and he meant to keep it.

Such is the louche background to "Good-Bye to the Mezzogiorno," in which Auden calls himself one of those who've come south "hoping to twig from / What we are not what we might be next." Meanwhile, the less spiritually ambitious—Chester?—believe erotic opportunities to be better here, "and much cheaper / (Which is doubtful)." Perhaps neither cheaper nor better. And anyhow,

> . . . *between those who mean by a life a*
> Bildungsroman *and those to whom living*
> *Means to-be-visible-now, there yawns a gulf*
> *Embraces cannot bridge.*

I've been as awed as the next non-Mediterranean by the effortless young eroticism, the being-visible-now, the quasi-divinity that flows from a fundamentally theatrical sense of life. These olive-skinned, black-eyed godlings go into the street to be seen. Grant them their season, it will be short. On the quay, I observe an elderly toper balancing a bottle on his head, and tell myself that this is Giocondo.

From Pithekoussai the Greekness spread. Hera, queen of the gods, was worshipped here as the guardian of success-ful voyages and new cities, though tradition saw her as likelier to wreak vengeance than to nurture. What tough-mindedness, what daring to petition the likes of Hera, who'd as soon see ships drowned and cities razed. But such was the Archaic religios-ity, as we know it from Homer: to posit divinities that are beyond good and evil inasmuch as they are but names for the inescap-able realities of nature. "How else could this people, so sensitive, so vehement in its desires, so singularly capable of *suffering*," asks Nietzsche, "have endured existence, if it had not been revealed to them in their gods, surrounded by a higher glory?" Hera is mar-riage, marriage bed, motherhood, and the chafing against those confinements; Zeus, the thunderbolt out of the mountain and the weather-world it stands for; his daughter Athena, the cun-ning to prevail in combat, and skill to excel at the loom or pot-ting wheel; Aphrodite, the glamour and devastation of desire; Ares, her consort, the brute inevitability of war; Artemis, the safeguards of chastity and the hazards of childbirth; her brother Apollo, the art of healing and the ruthlessness of disease; Posei-don, the bounty and peril of the sea. These Greek immortals embody things one cannot *not* believe in. Thus their advantage over the Jewish or Christian godheads. (Hats off to the latter for being tripartite, and hats off to medieval traditions for extending the worship to Mary and all the saints. But the best polytheism knows itself for what it is, and such frankness Roman Catholics will never tolerate, unmistakably polytheistic though their devotion is.) The Homeric gods are a glorifying mirror in which the mutability of nature and of ourselves is found again—immortally joyous, forever shining. "These Greek gods," wrote Norman Douglas, "are extra-human rather than super-human: they are interpenetrations of human motives with new and unaccountable elements." What a good religion, that extinct one, superior by far to the variously self-deceiving confessions practiced round the world today.

Years ago, I checked into Buddhism (attractively atheistical), attempted to read the Koran, spent the weekend at an ashram in the Berkshires, even went to Catholic mass and received the Host (shameful thing to have done). The premise of this shopping around was clear: any faith but the one I was raised in. Sensing my folly, and perhaps knowing how to end it, my friend David Hadas, of blessed memory, put me onto a book that his father, the renowned classicist and erstwhile rabbi Moses Hadas, had translated, Walter Otto's *The Homeric Gods*. A revelation. Here was someone *arguing for*, not just studying, the varieties of Greek religious experience. I bought in. "The gods retain their own existence," Otto writes, "from which man is by his nature forever kept apart. . . . Of this there can be no doubt: that such gods could have no thought of redeeming man from the world and raising him to themselves." A religion of things as they brutally are, a religion devoid of wishful thinking— that was and is for me.

Villa Arbusto, which houses the archaeological museum at Lacco Ameno, on the north shore of Ischia, is my destination this wintry morning. I want to stare at one object in particular, the Coppa di Nestore—Nestor's Goblet. Readers of the *Iliad* will remember that Nestor, wisest of the Achaeans, counselor to Agamemnon, possessed a drinking vessel of chased bronze set with gold, a cup so heavy it took a hero to lift it (though Nestor could lift it with ease). From the road, Villa Arbusto looks as shut up as a sleeping fruit bat. I have been assured by telephone that the museum is APERTO till noon. I trudge up the hill to find CHIUSO on the door. I lose my temper and begin to pound. They are too much, these people. (The phrase "these people," ever popular with Anglo-Saxons on tour, has a tendency to pop out of me more than I like.) I pound. An elderly stalwart of the place opens up, ready to give me an earful, I can see. I state my case. She shakes her head firmly. I persist: *"Solo per vedere la Coppa, signora. Per piacere."* Nothing doing. Then I unknowingly utter the open sesame that grants immediate passage into realms of the CHIUSO, the IN RESTAURO, the VIETATO: *"Sono professore, signora."* She bows her head, steps back from the door to let me pass. (This Italian reverence for professional titles is touching to all who've observed it. Primo Levi describes how, after his capture in Valle d'Aosta by Fascists, a militiaman who'd beaten him begged pardon later, saying he hadn't known the prisoner was *un dottore.* "Italy," Levi writes, "is a strange country.")

The lights of the museum are switched on for me. My eye goes straight to the Goblet. It's smaller than I'd expected, and without much pride of place. *"Molto importante per noi,"* the custodian murmurs as we stare. It sounds perfectly natural in her language, but when I imagine myself showing off some American object—Washington's weather vane at Mount Vernon, or Lincoln's top hat at the Smithsonian, or FDR's pince-nez at Hyde Park— and saying, "This is very important to us," well, I just don't feature myself saying that. Perhaps the material remains of our civilization aren't old enough. There's a pathos more and more accruing to things the more ancient they become. At any rate, the highest goose-flesh I ever got in North America was at the cliff dwellings of Mesa Verde, because it was *twelfth*-century Americans who built them.

Nestor's Goblet dates from the eighth century B.C., the century of Homer. It was the century, also, in which Greeks acquired the alphabet—one of the most transforming technologies ever devised, incalculable, really, in its consequences—and the Greeks, having acquired it, passed alphabetism on to Etruria and Rome and thence to all of Europe.

The way to the alphabet is unimaginably arduous, a struggle of the practical intellect akin to figuring out how to sail the seas. Pictograms, representations of the thing referred to, were human-kind's earliest attempt to write, followed by ideograms, stylizations only partly representational, followed in their turn by phonograms, signifiers entirely released from representation of the signified. The momentous next step is to an endlessly recombinable system of consonants and vowels, a leap analogous to the advance from arithmetic to algebra.

All the early systems of writing we know—Sumerian cuneiform, Egyptian hieroglyphics, Minoan Linear A, Mycenaean Linear B— settled for some combination of the ideographic and pictographic. As to *alphabetic* writing, it had its Levantine genesis in the Bronze Age Near Eastern cities of Byblos and Ugarit, where merchants in need of a rapid means of certifying contracts and accounts receivable seem to have retooled the old cuneiform signs to function more efficiently as unlimited combinations of a strictly limited consonant-and-vowel system. And though they did not feel the earth shake when they did so, the earth did shake.

Our earliest instance of these Syrian ABC's is datable to the fourteenth century B.C. At about the same time, in Canaan, a different linear alphabet was coming into use, and on it the varieties of Semitic literacy would be based. But it is the Phoenicians who streamlined the new technology and handed it on to Hellas. This happened only at the turn of the eighth century B.C., perhaps at Al-Mina, a Phoenician and subsequently Greek commercial center on the Levantine coast, in present-day Turkey. So the historical moment in which the oral bard Homer sang is the same moment in which Greeks first acquired the means of writing down his song.

As for the Goblet at Villa Arbusto, bearing perhaps the earliest alphabetic inscription we have in Greek, it turns out to be a humbler item than its Homeric prototype. "Whoever drinks from me will get a hard-on," says Ischia's *molto importante* cup.

Connected to Ischia by a narrow bridge is Castello Aragonese, the vast fortress that served a succession of occupiers—Syracusans, Romans, Parthenopeans, Visigoths, Vandals, Ostrogoths, Saracens, Normans, Swabians, and Angevins. When Monte Epomeo erupted for the last time, in 1301, Ischians took refuge here. A century and a half later, under Alfonso V of Aragon, king of Naples, it provided shelter from marauding pirates. In the early sixteenth century, Vittoria Colonna—poet, *salonnière*, muse, glamour girl, religious recluse—married Ferrante d'Avalos, Marquis of Pescara, at the church within the castle walls. Hers was quite a roster of cavaliers: Michelangelo, Ariosto, Bernardo Tasso, Aretino, Bembo, and Sannazaro all danced attendance. Today, I wander down to the Olive Terrace, once Vittoria's private garden, and behold, lumbering like a B-52 into the bright air, a peacock. He alights on a parapet—doubtless the place where he knows he looks best—and poses there, revolving something in his minuscule brain. Then he opens his fan. Suns and moons shimmer iridescently in the morning light. I come closer, but he leaps down and disappears into the brush.

Michelangelo said of Vittoria Colonna that she was both man and woman and thereby divine—*"un uomo in una donna, anzi un dio."* Sufficient to call her one of the most remarkable women of the Italian Renaissance. Had the labyrinthine political intrigues of the 1520s played out another way, she might well have reigned not just here on Ischia but over there at Naples, for her husband's ambitions extended that far, and his deft management of Holy Roman Imperial, Spanish, and French belligerents might have gained him the Neapolitan throne. In the event, chatelaine of Ischia was what Vittoria remained, from which fastness she watched the savage power struggles. "Just as Phoebus confers more radiance upon his white sister the Moon . . ." sings Ariosto in *Orlando furioso*, "so he gives such power to this lady's lofty words that in our day he has adorned heaven with another sun. Victoria is her name." After Ferrante's death (he is interred at Naples, in San Domenico Maggiore),

Castello Aragonese, Ischia Ponte

she wrote poems to sanctify him, which, even if Ariosto declares that they rescue "her triumphant spouse from the dark shore of the Styx to make him gleam in the firmament," are pretty heavy going; spent reflective time in various conventual orders; and conferred with the geniuses of the age. When in 1547 she died at Rome, Michelangelo was by her side.

From windows at the Donjon, the castle within Castello Aragonese, where Vittoria lived intermittently, she had a view to Procida and beyond to Campi Flegrei, the headland west of Naples. At Pozzuoli, a volcanic crater—the Solfatara—emits impressive *fumaroli,* jets of mud, sand, and steam. At Agnano is a sulfurous cave, the Grotta del Cane, into which local hucksters in the era of the Grand Tour would throw dogs, causing them to appear to die. One eighteenth-century English traveler writes: "The poor animal who is now undergoing the experiment . . . has already been three years at it, and, at a moderate computation, he has been killed a hundred times a year. . . . Upon being brought again into the air, his lungs begin to play violently, and in four or five minutes' time he is perfectly recovered." Nearby is the Astroni crater, several miles in circumference. A royal hunting ground under the Bourbons, it is today among the loveliest nature preserves in southern Italy. Birds nest abundantly in poplars, oaks, chestnuts, and elms. Baia (Baiae), also nearby, was in Roman times the world's choicest watering place, an ancient Costa Smeralda. Denounced by Seneca for its monstrous opulence and supposed depravity, the ancient town is now in large part underwater, a result of volcanic undulations; this geologically turbulent terrain is called Campi Flegrei—Burning Fields—for good reason. The Greeks believed that the Olympian gods had imprisoned their predecessors, the Titans, underground, and the roiling earth was proof of their presence. At Campi Flegrei you were nearer to darkness and old night.

In Cumae (modern-day Cuma) is what is traditionally honored as the cave where, according to Virgil, the frenzied Sibyl made her vaticinations, then wrote them down:

> *Ashore there, when you reach the town of Cumae,*
> *Avernus' murmuring forests, haunted lakes,*
> *You'll see a spellbound prophetess, who sings*
> *In her deep cave of destinies, confiding*
> *Symbols and words to leaves. Whatever verse*
> *She writes, the virgin puts each leaf in order*
> *Back in the cave; unshuffled they remain;*
> *But when a faint breeze through a door ajar*
> *Comes in to stir and scatter the light leaves,*
> *She never cares to catch them as they flutter. . . .*

It is how she's been seen ever since, wild-eyed amid the storm of her previsions. The semi-legendary last king of Rome, the Etruscan Tarquinius Superbus, is said to have gone to her to purchase the nine books containing her prophecies. The price she quoted him being exorbitant, he refused. She destroyed three of them, then offered the remaining six at the same high price. When he again refused, she destroyed three more. She offered the remaining three, still at no discount, and he agreed, brought them to Rome, and deposited them in the temple to Jupiter on the Capitoline Hill.

Whatever their real origins, and however they actually did come to Rome, the civic role of the Sibylline Books was preeminent throughout republican and into imperial times. Consulted by a select few, they were believed to prescribe, in Greek, religious practices necessary to avert pestilence, earthquakes, comets, and so forth. What the Books accomplished, in reality, was a Hellenization of the indigenous Roman beliefs and usages—a process already begun through Roman contact with Hellenes and Hellenized Etruscans—through the introduction of new gods and new cults and the consequent transfiguring of Rome's existing pantheon and ways of worship.

At Cuma, the limestone "cave" of the Sibyl, a gallery cut in the usual trapezoidal way, had been in Greek times a defensive corridor to the acropolis beneath which the actual Cavern of the Sibyl seems to have been located. The surrounding park has been fitted out, courtesy of Mussolini, with plaques on which relevant passages from the *Aeneid* are quoted in the original, meant to prepare you for the cave, I guess, in the way salacious images at the *luparia* of Pompeii would get a fellow ready for love. With Virgil's poetry ringing in your ears, go stand alone some morning in that limestone corridor and you will give yourself the willies, even though no sibyl ever raved there.

By the eastern shore of Lake Avernus, traditional point of access to realms of the dead, Emperor Hadrian in the second century built a temple to Apollo (a thermal hall, really) whose dimensions were nearly those of the Pantheon in Rome. Its ruins remain. Tradition holds that the lake itself is so mephitic that no bird can fly across it and live, though I watched a flock of birds do just that, then took out again my copy of Robert Fitzgerald's translation of the *Aeneid*, better here than any guidebook. Aeneas has asked of the Sibyl that he be allowed to go to the dead and see his father, Anchises. Her response seems to me one of the best things in all of literature: "Black Dis's door stands open night and day." It is easy to die, in other words; arrange it for any hour—the dose of poison, the leap into thin air, what you will. But to go down to the dead and come again among the living, that's hard. Never dream of doing so, unless you carry as your safeguard the Golden Bough. At a gorge of the lakeside, Aeneas plucks it up, "bright amid the dark green ilex," and carries it back to the Sibyl's lair. Only then does she, surest of necromancers, consent to lead him to "the deep world sunk in darkness under the earth," where the generations of the dead are seen and the generations of the unborn foreseen. His father's shade says:

> *What glories follow Dardan generations*
> *In after years, and from Italian blood*
> *What famous children in your line will come,*
> *Souls of the future, living in our name,*
> *I shall tell clearly now, and in the telling*
> *Teach you your destiny.*

There in Hades, Aeneas is at the quick. To see oneself as historical, a moment in the cavalcade or a link in the chain—what greater fullness of life can there be than that longest view? Clothed in the seriousness of the ages, you are not only yourself. To think and feel thus historically seems to me the one durable stance. Still, it can be only retrospective. Walter Benjamin says of the angel of history, his allegorical figure of historical consciousness, that while his face is turned to the past, a strong wind out of paradise drives him forward, and that what he beholds is wreckage on wreckage, human events piling up to the skies. Sad Aeneas sees all that too and, granted the burden of future sight, sees what the angel of history cannot: the wreckage to come.

There is a Naples of sunlight and noise, and another, virtually coextensive with it, of pitch-darkness and silence. That nether-Naples, a vast honeycomb of mines, reservoirs, aqueducts, cisterns, caverns, grottoes, galleries, hypogea, catacombs, and rough-hewn cathedrals, is visitable only in part. It was the Greeks who originally hollowed out—one block of calcareous yellow tufa at a time—these subterranean realms. As the city grew, so did the undercity, this obverse or negative image. The stones of Naples are light and porous, ideal for building. Slaves cut them from the subterranean chambers and hoisted them to the surface through shafts. And there had been considerable quarrying by an indigenous people preceding the Greeks whose evidences go back to Neolithic times; the very earliest so far, excavated in the Materdei quarter about twenty-five years ago, is a pair of tombs dating from 5000 B.C. (At Syracuse, the famous *latomie,* deep limestone pits into which, at a turning point of the Peloponnesian War, the defeated Athenians were thrown to die of hunger and thirst, are similarly Neolithic in origin.) Neapolitan Greeks themselves doubted that primitive people could have accomplished such feats of quarrying, and ascribed the grottoes to mythic Cimmerians—according to Homer, a race of men who craved darkness as others sought light and who lived near the House of the Dead.

You read of foolhardy Victorian schoolmasters leading their charges into that pitch-dark labyrinth, never to return. When occupying German forces suddenly retreated from Naples in September of 1943, it was feared by the populace that their retreat was a feint and that hundreds of thousands more were massed underground for miles on end, waiting to leap forth like Achaeans from the wooden horse. Such an underworld is a great generator of myths and a great incitement to mythic emotions. Down there for an afternoon, inching along one of the narrow courses between reservoirs, my guide—my necromancer—going before me with a candle, I wonder aloud what would happen if a sudden gust should blow it out. *"Ho sempre una torcia,"* he assures me. He always has a flashlight. *"Non è che per fare effetto, la candela."* The candle is only for effect. Be that as may be; though in the wavering light there is no Eurydice to look back on, he is Hermes, god of guidance and inventor of fire and firesticks. And I must be Orpheus, self-flattering though this is.

The ancient system of aqueducts through which we meander, forced sometimes to wriggle sidewise through the sluiceways, had remained in use till the horrendous Asiatic cholera of 1884, a sudden devastation spread by sewage-polluted water. Whereas the nineteenth-century aristocrats and bourgeoisie of the upper town drank filtered rainwater from cisterns, the inhabitants of the lower town—*il ventre di Napoli*, the underbelly of Naples, as Matilde Serao called it—drew a fetid, stinking brew from the ancient reservoirs, or even ghastlier swill from derelict courtyard wells. "Such water is evil," one medical health officer reported at the outbreak of the epidemic, "not only because of filthy seepage but also on account of the solid materials floating within it." Once the cholera took hold, it was their deaths people were hoisting up at the wellheads of the lower town.

Drained and sealed off from water sources as part of the Risana-
mento, the urban renewal undertaken after the epidemic, the now
dry *sotterranea* became a vast garbage dump. For half a century Neapolitans threw their refuse down the old wells. Then, in November
of 1940, British bombers began their attacks on port installations.
For the next thirty-four months, Naples would be a recurrent Allied
target. The generations of subterranean garbage were hurriedly
tamped down and paved over, and the aqueducts fitted up for shel-
ters. Large numbers of people actually lived in them for weeks or
more. There are frightening graffiti down there, along with the
makeshift beds, toy cars, sewing machines, chamber pots. On one
wall are line drawings of Hitler and the Duce in profile, and beneath
them a crude rendering of the globe inscribed with "VINCE-
REMO" ("We will win"); on another, "MAMMA NON PIANGE"
("Mama doesn't cry"); on another, what looks like a child's drawing of a bomb, and the single word "AIUTO" ("Help"). "Lady, be
good," says my Hermes to the flickering flame.

"You know about the *Lady Be Good*, Professore?" It was, he tells
me, the name an American flight crew had given to their Liberator,
one of a squadron that bombed Naples. He tells me the tale without a hint of reproach. His overwhelming admiration for all things
American, including our destructive know-how, is evident. Like
everyone here—and I mean everyone—he has a relative in America.
Like nearly everyone under a certain age, he wants to immigrate there
himself ("Is the best country"). The men of the *Lady Be Good* had
dropped their payload on Naples harbor, then got hopelessly lost on
the return to North Africa. Believing themselves still over the Mediterranean, they had in fact flown hundreds of miles into the Libyan

Desert before their engines sputtered and all hands bailed out. The men wandered the wastes south of Tobruk, perishing one by one. In 1960, a diary was discovered, along with several skeletons. "No signs of *anything*," wrote one of the dying men, "a couple of birds; good winds from N.—Really weak now, can't walk, pains all over, still all want to die. Nites very cold, no sleep."

The most dreadful of the Greek gods, Ares, never done with his harvest of lives, is loathed by divinities and mortals alike. Whereas Thanatos can claim his inevitable share in nature, Ares remains the eternal aberration, unnatural however hardy and ever-green. "He is the spirit of imprecation, vengeance, blood-guilt," says Walter Otto. "His element is manslaughter." Ares' son is the dragon slain by Cadmus, who, when he sows the dragon's teeth in the earth, causes the first army to spring up. Cadmus placates Ares by marrying his daughter Harmony, and at their wedding feast gods and mortals dine together for the last time. "These things never happened, but are always," says Sallust. (There may somewhere be a profounder remark about myths in general, but I don't know it.) Cadmus, inventor of armies, is also credited by the Greeks with inventing the alphabet. The same cunning, in other words, that devises the engines of history devises a technology for preserving the account—the *logos*—of what those engines have brought forth. With the marriage of Cadmus and Harmony, Thebes is founded, civil order secured, bloody-mindedness overcome . . . Like fun it is. The house of Cadmus, like our house in history, is a charnel. I therefore prefer the simpler myth about Ares being imprisoned in a

*Remains of crew member
of the* Lady Be Good, *1960*

brazen barrel and Hermes the trickster arriving to release him—which favor the god of
war, however despised, may count on till the
end of time.

Now my Hermes releases me. We mount
the four hundred stairs to the lit world. I
thank him, pay him, and walk blindly into
via dei Tribunali. Without premeditation,
thinking just to rest my sun-struck eyes,
I enter the Church of San Lorenzo Maggiore, where—against tradition, principles,
reason, and good sense—I am all at once
praying, though I know not to Whom, for souls of Naples and of
the *Lady Be Good* and, as it cannot hurt, for all of us.

TWO

Four Europes

They always come, the gods. They will descend
from their machines, and some they'll save,
others they will violently, suddenly raise
by the middle; and when they've brought some order
they will withdraw. —And then this man will do this,
and that man that; and in time the others
will do as they see fit. And so we will start over.

—C. P. Cavafy, "The Intervention of the Gods"

*Y*ou *may dig around Caesar Augustus* all you like
and not unearth him. Better documented than most anyone
from antiquity, the man who found Rome a city of brick and mortar
and left it a city of marble withholds the secret of his nature. All
acknowledge his extraordinary luck in being named Julius Caesar's
adopted son, and his skill at marrying above his rank. A simplicity
of living by comparison with *bon viveurs* all about him is universally praised: he preferred a little fish or meat with black bread and
a modicum of wine to the usual hearty patrician intake, and kept,
in addition to a villa at Capri, but three other retreats, at Lanuvium
(Lanuvio), Tibur (Tivoli), and Praeneste (Palestrina). As to quarters in town, those lucky enough to have visited "Livia's House" on

the Palatine will have noted how sweetly human-scale the dimensions are. It was there that Augustus and his empress lived when in Rome.

And alongside the simplicity, the brutality. The young Octavius who'd marched on Rome at eighteen had a vein of iron in him that showed as brutally in the mature Augustus. True enough, after the battle of Actium, when the last of his enemies were vanquished, he cultivated a public image of judicious mercy. After the battle of Philippi eleven years earlier, on the other hand, he'd ordered the severed head of Brutus to be placed at the base of Julius Caesar's statue. ("The buzzards will take care of that," Suetonius reports him as saying.) Perhaps the most damning item in the dossier remains Augustus's treatment of Julia, his only biological child, exiled to the godforsaken island of Pandateria (modern-day Ventotene) for her enterprising sex life. Well documented though it is, there remains for no less a historian than Ronald Syme the strong suspicion that Augustus made a convenience of Julia's waywardness in order to eliminate, for reasons of his own, certain of the men who'd happened to enjoy her favors. As more or less every mother's son *had* been to bed with her, real and imagined adversaries could go to the wall as Augustus chose.

And poor Julia was one of the most appealing personalities of the age. Asked how she managed to have children who resembled her husbands instead of her lovers, she said she took new passengers on board only once the hold of the ship had been loaded. Any wit capable of that deserves better than Pandateria.

A curious glimpse into the character of Augustus is provided by the historian Cassius Dio in his account of a banquet at the lavish villa of one Vedius Pollio: Pausilypon, or Pause from Care. (The northern reach of the Neapolitan Bay is to this day called Posillipo.) Vedius's pleasure palace covered much of the headland, and surviving ruins of outlying structures—amphitheater, odeon, nymphaeum, temple, and so on—give an idea of Pausilypon's splendor. Its proprietor was known to be the cruelest of men. He kept a pond stocked with man-eating lampreys, into which he would throw menials who displeased him. At the banquet for Caesar Augustus, Vedius ordered wine to be served in crystal goblets, one of which shattered on the pavement. The manservant responsible was instantly condemned to the lampreys, whereupon Augustus ordered the rest of the goblets thrown to the pavement and, rounding on his horrified host, asked, "How then will you punish me?"

One cannot thoroughly dislike the man who ordered Vedius's goblets smashed. Or who, as he lay dying, asked those present if they had enjoyed the play. Or who, meeting a man in foreign parts who resembled him, asked, "Was your mother ever in Rome?" and laughed heartily when the man bested him by saying, "No, *princeps*, but my father often was." Like many another genius of power, he bewilderingly combines inhumanity with charm.

The story of the goblets is part of a considerable lore concerning ancient Romans on the Bay of Naples. It was their Hamptons, their Cape and Islands, their Penobscot Bay. From the time of the initial Romanization after the Second Samnite War, the mighty of Rome built villas here in a landscape of matchless beauty and a cultural surround of refined and exotic Greekness. It was precisely this difference from Rome that beguiled them. Romans revered the Hellenic nature of Naples and wished to preserve it. Accordingly, where other Greek cities did not survive as such, Naples did—Greek in speech, art, architecture, manners, and habit of mind—right up to the collapse of the Western Empire in the fifth century.

When that empire did finally fall, Odoacer, king of the Goths, sent the last emperor, Romulus Augustulus, to Campania, imprisoning him in what had once been the sumptuous Villa of Lucullus. From the Middle Ages forward it was the site of the Castel dell'Ovo, which guarded Virgil's Egg, ancient palladium of the city, on which its destiny depended. It's as if fate took a hand in this last emperor's name, combining as it does that of the legendary founder of Rome, Romulus, with the name of the historic bringer of the Pax Romana, Augustus.

Deposed by Odoacer, Romulus Augustulus lingered out his days here. You may descend to the depths of Castel dell'Ovo to view what remains of Lucullus's *domus*, foundations repeatedly built over from the twelfth century on. What his house may have been is best conjectured from Roman villas that survive marvelously well as a result of the great eruption of Vesuvius in 79. Strabo describes the shoreline as a necklace of residential splendors running unbroken from Misenum all the way round to what is now Punta della Campanella. Vesuvius had not erupted in historic times, though we know it to have been ferocious in the Paleolithic and Neolithic. It was merely picturesque to the Romans who built in its shadow. The Bay was for them the pause from care pure and simple, not the reminder of mortality it has been from the third quarter of the first century. For example, at Oplontis (modern-day Torre Annunziata) is the admirably excavated Villa of Poppaea. Much less visited than the sights of Pompeii or Herculaneum, it merits an afternoon of its own. The grounds have been planted with the vegetation that would have adorned such a house. The peristyle is intact. The structures are roofed. Everything about the site is comprehensible; one truly senses, as so seldom at archaeological sites, what it felt like to walk those grounds, enter those rooms.

The dimensions, inferable from the portion excavated, along with the extraordinary quality of the wall paintings, lead strongly to the conclusion that this was the Campanian retreat of no less a Poppaea than Nero's second wife, whose coronation Claudio Monteverdi gives us sixteen centuries later in one of the world's first and most beautiful operas, *L'incoronazione di Poppea*. Murderess of anyone who got in her way, Poppaea Sabina has found no advocate among historians ancient or modern, but she did with Monteverdi's librettist Giovanni Francesco Busenello. (Opera, a late Renaissance innovation seeking to recapture the lost musical dimension of Greco-Roman drama, inevitably began with classical subject matter; Monteverdi's three surviving operas—at least fifteen other works lost to fire at Mantua—are *L'Orfeo*, *Il ritorno di Ulisse in patria*, and *L'incoronazione*.) Busenello's Poppea is first and last a woman in love, and psychopathic only when necessary. She was a worthy match for Nero, who kicked her to death in the year 65, according to Suetonius, then stuffed her body with spices and displayed it in the Mausoleum of Augustus.

Monteverdi's late masterwork was among the first operas I ever saw, in a Met production on tour at the State Fair Music Hall in Dallas. A gentleman of the old school, Abe "Fischy" Fischbein, invited me to go with him. Mr. Fischbein was learned and kind. I'd been over to his house to listen to records and talk about books. He was, I understand now, one of those cultivated men who from the purest of motives love sharing their knowledge and passion with children. Life at the Fischbeins' seemed to me one long symposium. You heard things not heard at our house. Mr. Fischbein said music was the mother art, more ancient even than image-making or architecture. I was eleven, a little young for such tenets, but he told me that all the arts reconcile our senses to our intelligence and that all art, even when it is very sad art, celebrates that reunion. (Years later, when I came upon the Renaissance musicologist Gioseffo Zarlino's definition of music as a mingling of "the incorporeal energy of reason with the body," I felt that Mr. Fischbein was speaking to me again.) He said that music intimates everything we gained by becoming human—brainpower, creativity, self-reflection, wisdom born of beauty. He had two good-looking, dynamic daughters a little older than I, but liked, I think, imparting these high-flown things to a boy. And I may have been the only one for miles around who responded. And Mr. Fischbein, God bless him, liked me without liking me too much. Anyhow, off to *L'incoronazione* we went. I had never till that night heard of the Emperor Nero, or of Claudio Monteverdi. *Madame Butterfly* was the limit of what I'd heard. I chiefly recollect the sets and the glassy, unfamiliar sound of the harpsichord. This was before supertitles, long before, and what I also remember is the fervor with which we applied ourselves beforehand to the plot synopsis, never good enough to give you a grasp of what you were to see. Never mind. Under Abe Fischbein's tutelage I became convinced that real life was the grandiose one unfolding up there onstage, and that our own down in the audience was a barren imposture.

Opera was but half a century old when Monteverdi composed his masterpiece. He'd been the presiding genius for all of opera's formidable early development, and at the end of his days brought it to the sublime. Listening to *L'incoronazione di Poppea* now, armed with what I know, I recognize the distinctive "style of old age," economical, fearless, effortlessly deep, miraculously new, as in Shakespeare's romances, Beethoven's final piano sonatas, Goya's black paintings, Verdi's *Falstaff*, Tolstoy's last stories, Yeats's *Last Poems*, Shostakovich's final string quartets: late style, in which the impulses of a creative lifetime are, in death's shadow, chastened, and the old perfections transfigured. Monteverdi seems, indeed, to have died not long after the premiere of *L'incoronazione*. A paradoxical blitheness is one hallmark of late style, and Monteverdi's masterwork is blithe even amid Nero's matter-of-fact butcheries. When at the urging of Poppaea he orders Seneca, his tutor from boyhood, to commit suicide, the great Stoic asks only that a warm bath be drawn and serenely goes off, as friends weep and wail, to open a vein and die. He needs no orders from the emperor, Mercury having appeared to him with the mortal tidings. "Now I confirm my writings," Seneca says, "I certify my studies. Leavetaking is a blessed fate when death issues from a mouth divine."

At Poppaea's house on the Bay, excavated at about ten meters below the street level of a gritty working-class exurb of Naples, you enter the generous atrium, its ceiling pierced by a square opening corresponding to the *impluvium*, or rain basin, in the floor, as at most Roman villas. But here the dimensions are royal, as confirmed by wide corridors, matched peristyles, luxurious baths, an exceptionally large swimming pool, numerous salons, dining rooms, bedrooms.

The wall paintings—which are what most people come to see—are exceptional. The best of Roman painting, very precious in itself, is also our best intimation of the lost wonders of Greek painting. According to Pliny the Elder, the Hellenic masters could paint curtains so illusionistic that even other artists would be tricked into trying to draw them back, and clusters of grapes so lifelike that the birds would come to peck at them. He says that certain artists could paint unpaintable things, such as thunder. Anyhow, most of the surviving wall paintings we have—chiefly from Pompeii and Herculaneum, and housed today at the Museo Archeologico Nazionale in Naples—are a very long way from this impossible standard. Was the author of the *Historia naturalis* marveling at easel and panel works, no example of which has survived?

There are, in any case, wall paintings of a very high realism to be seen at Vergina in northern Greece, at Pompeii's Villa of the Mysteries, and at the Museo Nazionale Romano at Palazzo Massimo in Rome—where Livia's radiant summer dining room, reassembled from her house at Prima Porta, is on view again after many years—to name just three examples. At Vergina, in Macedonia, on the wall of a little tomb within the so-called Great Tumulus, is a brilliantly executed Hades carrying away Persephone. At the Villa of the Mysteries are frescoes—instantly distinguishable from the "equivalent of bourgeois wallpaper," as classicist and historian Mary Beard characterizes the overall standard of Pompeii and Herculaneum—depicting initiation into the Dionysian Mysteries in scenes running continuously round the room. And at Villa Massimo, the mural similarly encompasses all four walls, interrupted only by the low doorway through which one enters a painted garden stretching away in every direction to woodlands, all of it alive with birds, rabbits, and other creatures, and vegetation of the most rigorous verisimilitude. Writing of this *triclinium* in 1960, before it vanished from view for more than a generation, Elizabeth Bowen observed in *A Time in Rome*: "The wood recedes, as in life, into veils of atmosphere:

everything in the forefront is in stereoscopic closeness to you—the veining of leaves, corollas uneven or dinted, the molded, tipped and directed feathers composing the characteristic plumage of each bird. . . . There is not a breeze but the greenery has a look of not perfect stillness: animate, it must breathe." You do begin to understand what Pliny was raving about. The leaves of a maple, lifted like a girl's bangs, make the breeze perceptible.

Here at Oplontis, Poppaea enjoyed in her time a later manner of wall painting, as formidably illusionistic, which scholars call the Second Style. (Another superb example of Second is the *cubiculum* taken from nearby Boscoreale and reassembled at New York's Metropolitan Museum of Art.) Poppaea's walls show a beautifully translucent glass bowl filled with apples, a veiled jar containing various fruits, a woven basket of ripe figs; also a variety of birds, ornithologically correct and sharply alive. The settings for these naturalistic elements are highly fanciful architectural motifs. Wall painting of the Second Style opened out a room into perspectives on all four sides. That nearly all of this painted architecture is, on examination, improbable or impossible has occasioned a good deal of scholarly comment. It would seem that the purpose of such decoration was to augment the real leisure (*otium*) of imperial houses with a fantastical, unbuildable leisure, a neverworld of *luxe, calme et volupté* beckoning from the walls. Within this utopian matrix, however, the painter sets fruits and flowers and creature life—nature as we know it, ripening and decaying. And masks of tragedy turn up more than once, *memento mori* interrupting the dream world.

Everyone who sees these few examples of superb classical painting remarks on their haunting similarity to the art of the Italian fifteenth century. Foreshortening, anatomizing, modeling in light and shade, and otherwise coming to grips with how the eyes actually see things, Paolo Uccello, Domenico Veneziano, Melozzo da Forlì, Andrea del Castagno, Piero della Francesca, Andrea Mantegna, Antonio del Pollaiuolo, and Botticelli recovered the vanished genius of Greco-Roman painting. The Vergina depiction of Hades recalls Melozzo's windswept *Christ in Glory* now at the Quirinal Palace in Rome, down to the dynamic treatment of the hair and drapery. Solemn stately faces at the Villa of the Mysteries seem in the manner of Mantegna, and put one explicitly in mind of those in the Camera degli Sposi of Mantua's Ducal Palace. Livia's *triclinium* looks as if Botticelli had taken a hand in the rendering of the foliage, so similar is its atmosphere to that of his *Primavera* at the Uffizi in Florence.

Poppaea's villa at Oplontis and others, preserved in the ash or lava of the Vesuvian calamity and unearthed at Boscotrecase, Stabiae, Herculaneum, and Pompeii in the course of the last three centuries, form a uniquely valuable, compelling, and horrific testimony. When Goethe first saw Pompeii, he shuddered at the thought of so much life all at once extinguished—but on a second viewing had to admit of the "mummified city" that "few disasters . . . have given such delight to posterity." Delight, I must say, that rather spoils me for the more purely intellectual pleasure of ruins less well preserved. I recall my first visit, many years ago now, to the Sorrentine Peninsula and my disappointment at the ruins of Pollius Felix's villa at Capo di Sorrento. Just stony rectangles in the earth, the bare foundations. It was a raw March morning, the *tramontana* blowing wetly, nastily, and nobody there but me and two Englishwomen. Rigorous sightseers, they paced out the rooms, speculated about where the sea level had been in classical antiquity, settled disagreements by appeal to their Touring Club Red Guide (than which there is no better, or will ever be). The elder of the two had hiccoughs.

That evening I saw them again in the *salone* of the Excelsior Vittoria, built around the time of Queen Victoria's accession and named for her, and famed for later visits from King Edward VII, Caruso, and others. The elder lady still had her hiccoughs. The companion was reading aloud to her. It might as well have been olden times, King Edward napping in one of the easy chairs nearby, Lillie Langtry or Alice Keppel crocheting at his side. "I've had these hiccoughs for three days!" the lady wailed, and put her face in her hands. I felt so sorry for her. I stepped up and said I knew a foolproof American method for getting rid of them. "Come ahead, then!" she barked. She was nobility of some kind. The staff kept calling her Lady So-and-So. I explained that she must stand and raise both arms over her head. I called for a glass of water. "With your permission, ma'am, I'm going to feed this to you one swallow at a time. Hands high, please." Twenty swallows later, her ladyship was cured. She invited me to their table the following two nights, and would not hear of my paying. The companion, who'd seemed so skeptical of a piece of American flotsam like me, turned out to be jolly—she had a gift for mimicry and did my own and other accents to the nines— and erudite, and recommended several of the best scholarly works, including *Neapolitan Baroque & Rococo Architecture* by Anthony Blunt. "Wicked man, definitive book," she said.

Between the refined virtuosity of Poppaea's painted walls and the rudimentary pictorial efforts within the catacombs of San

Gennaro at Capodimonte, you may take the measure of all that separates classical from paleo-Christian times here on the Bay. San Gennaro is one of three visitable catacombs, along with San Gaudioso and San Severo. But a visit to any or all of them is bound to mislead. The large-scale necropolises of Naples are far more numerous, and interlocked, and they spread out vastly in all directions. It has always been believed here that someone with courage enough could walk the winding forty or fifty underground miles from Capodimonte to Pozzuoli by way of narrow sluiceways, rocky basilicas, ancient aqueducts, reservoirs, and the miles and miles of catacombs, a millennium's worth cleft from the tufa—this netherworld as large as great Naples itself and home to Christians who shall rise again in the flesh as their god did. (The Latin word *catacumba* means "sleeping place": a brief doze, then the apocalyptic reveille.)

That labyrinth is, for me, a nightmare world not to be contemplated without panic fear of darkness, airlessness, lostness. Along with another fear I here confess: fear of Christianity. "I come to call not the righteous, but sinners to repentance," said Jesus to the Pharisees. And what has this meant in practical terms? A masochistic preoccupation with suffering, death, and putrefaction—those supposed proofs of our original sinfulness. Nor does the countervailing principle to original sin, i.e., redemption—that through faith we may cross over to eternal safety—make me shudder less. Some years ago in St. Louis, trying to understand the religious motives of a character in a novel I was writing, I had a conversation with Walter J. Ong, the Jesuit critic and philosopher, and had the temerity to ask exactly what happens, inwardly, when a faithful Catholic like him receives the Eucharist. I knew I was not behaving well, but

Father Ong bore with me, saying that while his senses informed him that the feast was of bread and wine and his reason informed him that the feast was of bread and wine, what Scripture said was, "Take, eat; this is my body," and "This is my blood of the new testament, which is shed for many for the remission of sins," introducing believers to a revealed universe superior to that of sense and reason.

It was about as good an answer as one could hope for. But Christianity is, in all its versions, an untragic view of life, and I fear it not just because I'm a Jew whose ancestors suffered dreadful things under the heel of its triumph, and dislike it not just because I'm an unbeliever; I fear and dislike it because it sets the flesh against the mind and denies the brevity of our expectation; because, in a word, it is so un-Greek. So un-Leopardian. And yet like other skeptics I reverence it for having produced its share and more of the best European art and music. While I dread, in general, the power of mythology to overawe reason, I cherish the power of works of art to overawe the senses, and would not be deprived of Michelangelo or J. S. Bach—or, for that matter, the rude and moldered paintings and mosaics here at San Gennaro's catacombs.

"Severamente vietato, signore!" a tour guide calls after me when, braving the unknown, I venture down an off-the-tour corridor. *"È pericolosissimo, signore. Vi prego."* Sulkily, I come back to the fold. Like paleo-Christian crypts beyond the walls of Rome, these at Naples were established around the middle of the second century after some prior use as upper-class pagan burial places. The earliest iconography, however, dates only from the early fourth, the century of Constantine. Already you see art heading off in the direction called medieval. Gone are the modeling in light and shade, the

accurately rendered bodies and draperies, the depictions of depth. Round-eyed and expressionless, the sainted dead stare back, hands raised stiffly in the gesture of blessing. Here the one thing needful is salvation, not beauty.

Of the many Oriental religions that Roman soldiery carried back from the East, Christianity emerged as the decisive victor. The Roman divinities were, in the end, driven from their pedestals. Christ and the saints established sole dominion. It is the most astounding extirpation in all of European history, and the most consequential.

To come to the catacombs of San Gennaro or to those outside Rome, to see the new myths newly triumphant—this ought to be one of the greatest of experiences. Instead, it strangles me as if the stench of rotting flesh were still in the air. Would I do any better at Jewish catacombs? Those in Rome are frustratingly difficult to visit. Augustus Hare reports descending at Vigna Randanini to find broad passages, painted peacocks, and funerary slabs adorned with the seven-branched candlestick. Something like these Jewish catacombs existed at Naples; we know this on the strength of archaeological finds near via Trivice that would seem to date from the fifth century. Jews of the Diaspora had flourished all around the littoral from at least the first century; Procopius of Caesarea, last historian of the ancient world, claims that they were prominent in the local slave trade, a role curtailed only at the end of the sixth century, when Pope Gregory the Great enjoined them from trafficking in Christian chattel. (So says Procopius, who says many true things but also many false.)

What intrigues most today at the San Gennaro catacombs is a grotto, allegedly sacred throughout the Christian Middle Ages to

Priapus, son of Dionysus and Aphrodite. Priapus? How could such a devotion have survived? I think that these rites must have been anodyne sexual get-togethers in a forsaken place, all catacombs being out of use by the early medieval period; and that people have convened in out-of-the-way spots for that sort of thing in every epoch; and that the venerable Christian pedigree of these catacombs probably added an additional thrill to whatever the devotees of Priapus did down here. A large phallic stone at the center of the room, carved in Greek and Hebrew, has prompted all kinds of hypotheses, but the words are pseudo-erudite gobbledygook, and the stone dates from no earlier than the Renaissance. Proponents of a more sober school furthermore deny that any phallic rites took place here, ever. But I don't believe them.

Priapus, a minor god among so many others, was near to hand, literally so, whereas the major twelve of the Greek pantheon might well seem intimidatingly remote. Remoter still was a thirteenth of that pantheon, The Unknown God, as Greeks called him. Speaking at Athens on the Areopagus, the Hill of Ares, opposite the Acropolis, with its sanctuary of Zeus and temple to Athena, Paul of Tarsus declared that he had come to give a name to that Unknown God, make near what had been unreachable. Christianity named the unknown god and banished all others. And yet there were those who continued to perform the old sacrifices and, presumably, to feel the same emotions as their pagan forebears, even into the sixth, seventh, and eighth centuries, when it had become very dangerous and very peculiar to do so. There were, moreover, crypto-polytheists who, despite being baptized, continued to adhere in secret to the old plurality of gods. (They have their obvious analogues: baptized

Jews whose hidden practice continued to be Jewish; converts to Islam who remained secretly Christian.)

It is said that Christianity did not destroy the Greco-Roman gods, only drove them into hiding. The ruses by which polytheism survived were not so much in secret covens sustaining the old devotions as by *metamorphoses*—Cybele into the Virgin Mary, and Dionysus into Christ, and the translation of numberless local deities into local saints. In Greco-Roman religion, as in Christianity, the sacred was simultaneously far-off and nearby, the divinities innumerably present, local to human experience. Every city and town required its patron and intercessor, someone familiar to petition in a crisis. All who have visited the cathedral at Syracuse on one of the holy days when the silver effigy of Saint Lucy is brought forth will recall the wrought-up cry of the faithful: *"È siracusana!"* As much as to say, She's one of us. Afraid of the Father? Pray to the Son. Afraid of the Son? Pray to the Mother. Afraid of the Mother? Pray to your local deity. As in Christianity, so in paganism: Minor gods, familiar gods, special-use gods, customized gods have abounded. More than one parish at Naples seems to tolerate spontaneous devotion to some non-saint or other—typically a dead girl from the neighborhood—whom people believe sanctified and petitionable. As in the pagan past, so in the Christian present: New gods are always aborning.

None of this, of course, is how the triumphant Church of the late fourth and early fifth centuries understood itself. After the brief reign (361–363) of Julian the Apostate—polytheism's Indian summer—Theodosius I, last emperor to rule in both the West and the East of the empire, had made Christianity the official Roman religion and outlawed all others. It is frightening to read about the mob justice meted out in those decades—the temple of Serapis at Alexandria, a marvel, pulled down by Christian thugs in 391; North African cities terrorized by Circumcellions, martyrdom-loving monks who attacked people at random in the nihilistic hope of guaranteeing their own sanctification; monastic vigilantes in the north of Egypt conducting raids on houses suspected of harboring pagan sentiments or pagan idols; the philosopher Hypatia of Alexandria murdered by a gang of monks in 415, her flesh "scraped from her bones with sharp oyster shells," as Gibbon reports, "her quivering limbs . . . delivered to the flames." Such holy men were the jihadis of their day. Later, Eastern Emperor Theodosius II, observing adherents to the ancestral faith at their festivals, libations, and sacrifices, fulminates as follows: "A thousand terrors of the laws that have been promulgated, the penalty of exile that has been threatened, do not restrain them, but straightway they sin with such audacious madness!"

About a century and a half after that, under Justinian I, emperor of the East and reconqueror of the West as far as North Africa and southern Spain, pagans were everywhere still to be dealt with. Mutilation, beheading, and crucifixion were his methods, and these persecutions far exceeded the worst horrors faced by early Christians under Nero in the first century or Diocletian in the third.

So loyalists hung on tenaciously to the ways of the ancients, brave in the service of their gods. But even longer-lived is the whole skein of *unwitting* fidelities to the vanquished tradition. From the early fourth century, Christians who gathered at the catacombs of San Gennaro did so to be near the mortal remains of their wonder-working patron saint, martyred under Diocletian in the arena at Puteoli, as tradition has it, and eventually brought here for interment, where he remained for several centuries before being removed to the Duomo. Whether the faithful knew it or not, when they came to these catacombs and stayed the night, seeking communication with the saint through visions and dreams, they were enacting a traditional rite of incubation known throughout the Greek- and Latin-speaking world in pagan times. As medieval Christians would sleep at the basilica of Tours in the hope of being healed by Saint Martin, or at the abbey church of Conques to petition Sainte Foy, so they came to sleep, sometimes for many nights together, in the fifth-century basilica that stood above these Neapolitan catacombs, to commune with San Gennaro. Well insulated from the knowledge that what they were doing repeated the cultic past, they faithfully repeated it nonetheless; such testimony as we have of incubation at pagan shrines throughout the Roman Empire tallies with what we know of the Christian variety. Both involved feasting, singing, dancing, sleeping, and visions of the divine. Only the content of the visions differed, along with the powers beseeched. I offer incubation as one example—many others could be added—of how heathen usages, however thoroughly baptized, continued to pulse with their disavowed meanings. Call this the cunning of paganism.

Traces of the original basilica remain, though the church you see is overwhelmingly the result of a Fascist-era renovation. Go inside for a look at the fifth-century arch of the apse. But even this was not the first basilica of Naples. That was Santa Restituta, built in the reign of Constantine atop what had probably been a temple to Apollo, and incorporated in the fourteenth century into the Duomo. At a glance, what strikes you most there is the rococo decor dating from the seventeenth century. To the right of the apse a doorway takes you into San Giovanni in Fonte, the oldest surviving baptistery in Europe, once quite separate from Santa Restituta, it seems, but joined to it since late medieval times. The wonderfully refined mosaics are fifth-century, models of a paleo-Christian style still recognizably classical, as at Santa Pudenziana in Rome. They are doubtless much restored, and only four survive, in the most ruined of which nothing more than Saint Paul's legs appear. Another shows a man in a boat on a fish-thronged sea. A third shows Jesus standing on a globe as he hands the law to Peter. Fourth, and most memorable, are the Samaritan woman at the well and, cheek by jowl, the wedding feast at Cana; you can see the sloe-eyed rapture of two young men pouring out water from amphorae balanced on their shoulders as they observe it turning to wine; each registers the miracle by a contained gesture of the free hand. At the zenith of the cupola, directly above the basin, against a blue sky strewn with white and yellow stars, is the monogram of Christ, framed by an alpha and an omega signifying, of course, that he precedes and outlasts. But to come down from Christology to mere art history, these exquisite mosaics, pure works of the Western Empire, express an artistic omega and alpha; saying good-bye to classicism, they say hello to the devotional requirements of a new art.

The all-transforming fifth century, in which they were so lovingly executed, demonstrates the power of the unexpected in history.

> *Many are the forms of what is unknown.*
> *Much that the gods achieve is surprise.*
> *What we look for does not come to pass . . .*

The tragedies of Euripides often end with choric admonitions like this one from *Alcestis*. History, sings the chorus, turns out to be what nobody foresaw. The fifth and sixth centuries are defined by what nobody foresaw, the fall of the Western Roman Empire and the consequent transformation of Europe. Marx and Engels's 1848 formula for their own era is far more compelling as applied to the world of fifteen hundred years ago: "All that is solid melts into air, all that is holy is profaned, and man is at last compelled to face with sober senses his real conditions of life, and his relations with his kind." In about 370, a people of incomparable ferocity, the Huns, had appeared in Europe, driving everything before them. They'd made their way from north of the Great Wall of China, a journey of two hundred years. Now Germanic and Slavic tribes standing between them and Rome felt their fury. Thrown across the Dniester, Visigoths in turn drove Ostrogoths across the Danube and into Roman lands. Having learned from the Hunnish panoply—archers armed with the short bow and light lance on stirrup-driven horses— these Germanic tribes set about settling scores with Rome, a host they'd come to despise for past ill-treatment of their refugee populations: people rounded up into camps where they slowly starved to death, when not left to the tender mercies of the Hun. At Adrianople, the Goths handed Rome her worst rout since Carthage won at Cannae six centuries earlier. Adrianople was the beginning of the end. In the aftermath of this first defeat of Roman forces inside their borders, Vandals, Burgundians, Franks, Alemanni, Baiovari, Rugians, Alans, Suevi, Bulgars, Avars, and still obscurer peoples successively made their way into every part of the empire. It was thirty-two years later that Alaric and his Vandals sacked Rome. The defeat of Attila's Huns at the Catalaunian Fields in 451 only worsened matters, it seems, by taking the pressure off other nomadic armies. Odoacer, chief of the Heruli, entered Rome in 476, deposed Romulus Augustulus and sent him, as I say, to what had been the palace of Lucullus (later site of Castel dell'Ovo) in the harbor of Naples, thereby ending the Western Roman Empire. Twelve years afterward, acting at the instigation of Zeno, the Eastern emperor, Theodoric of the Ostrogoths invaded Italy, later capturing Ravenna from Odoacer. He invited him to dinner and sheared him in two. All of Italy was then Theodoric's. (If you go to Ravenna, his tomb is well worth a visit, a piece of pure Ostrogoth architecture owing nothing to either Rome or Constantinople.)

    E. H. Gombrich said of these vast migrations that they "swept up the Roman empire and whirled it to extinction." But not before one final attempt at restoring the *status quo ante*. That was the Eastern Emperor Justinian's nineteen-year campaign to wrest the Italian peninsula, North Africa, and southern Spain from Germanic hands. What this meant for Naples was two centuries of Byzantine rule, followed by an interregnum of Eastern hegemony alternating with local independence, and finally another four centuries of the independent duchy. Never was Naples the depopulated, shattered husk that Rome became in those times. When Vitiges the Goth cut the aqueducts in 537, the Eternal City contracted from the seven hills down to the Campus Martius along the Tiber, a bare encampment surrounded by the whistling empty grandeur of crumbling imperial edifices. "The lofty tree," Gibbon laments, "under whose shade the nations of the earth had reposed, was deprived of its leaves and branches, and the sapless trunk was left to wither on the ground." But if never depopulated, Naples was atrociously brutalized in those nineteen years of the Gothic contest with Justinian's armies and in the ravaging Lombard incursions that immediately followed. Not until the Second World War would the Bay know worse in the way of man-made horrors. The *casus belli* of this Gothic War, a barefaced pretext, is too tedious to narrate. Suffice it to say that around 534, in the seventh of his thirty-eight years as emperor of the East, Justinian embarked on the reconquest of Italy, a lifelong passion equaled only by the zest with which he strove to annihilate the remnants of Hellenism. His is the doubtful distinction of having torn down the academy originally founded by Plato at Athens.

Naples remained intact through the Gothic War, having bowed to Theodoric. In 536 came Belisarius, Justinian's fearsome general, as would-be liberator; Neapolitans sealed themselves up behind their walls, and it was only by means of a disused aqueduct that Byzantine forces breached and conquered the city. (Robert Graves vividly narrates this in his historical novel *Count Belisarius*.) The extent and position of Naples' Roman walls are conjectural; but six years later, we know, the Goths returned under the command of Totila, who tore them down in 543. Justinian dispatched his general Narses—a eunuch known as "The Hammer"—who nine years later, in his mid-seventies, defeated Totila at the battle of Taginae and a year after that annihilated the Goths altogether at the foot of Vesuvius. Within another two years he had driven the Alemanni and the Franks, who'd arrived in Italy to help the Goths, back over the Alps, then settled down to a sybaritic retirement on the Bay, dying at ninety-six in his villa here.

After the victories of Byzantium at Taginae and on the flank of Vesuvius, Naples again became a Greek-speaking city. Byzantine churches and monasteries took their place alongside Roman ones. But the menace of the Lombards, the latest in the bewildering

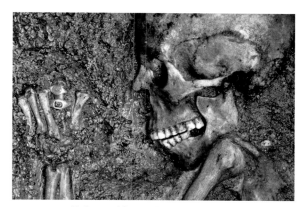

Skeleton with two rings, Herculaneum

Piazza del Plebiscito welcomes the Führer, May 5, 1938

Campanile of Pietrasanta

Detail of arcosolium
of Theotechnus family,
San Gennaro catacombs

The Martyrdom of Saint Ursula *by Caravaggio*

RIGHT:
The Seven Acts
of Mercy
by Caravaggio

Majolica cloister, Santa Chiara

Teatro San Carlo, from the third tier

Via Krupp, Capri

Villa Lysis, Capri

*Majolica pavement of
Leonardo Chiaiese,
Church of San Michele
Arcangelo, Anacapri*

Santa Chiara cloister

Cloud-set Monte Solaro, Capri

Tattered flyer for
Good Friday services
and Stations of the Cross,
Church of San Lorenzo Maggiore

Cast of Pompeiian
with Vesuvius
in the distance

Saint Matthew, detail of mosaic,
San Giovanni in Fonte, Duomo

Prometheus *by Jusepe de Ribera*

sequence of Germanic tribes invading the peninsula, was every-where. Scarcely a decade after taking Naples, Byzantium relin-quished it to these Longobardi, as they were known in Latin. Like the Goths immediately before them, they conquered most of Italy. Who were they? Another shaggy pastoral people, who started out from somewhere in Scandinavia about the time the Huns were start-ing out from Mongolia, and lived quietly for three hundred years along the lower course of the Elbe until, buffeted by the general panic the Huns produced, they settled first south and east of the Danube, then in Noricum and Pannonia (present-day Austria, Cro-atia, Hungary, and Slovenia). The Lombards stepped onto the stage of history when they broke loose from the *foederatus* within which Justinian had held them and, in alliance with Bulgars, Bavarians, Saxons, and Gepids, crossed the northeastern Alps to conquer, in short order, Vicenza, Verona, Brescia, and Milan, to give those cities their modern names. After a siege of three years, they took Pavia and made it their capital. (As to Venice, it did not yet exist, though this was the moment when the lagoon was first populated. The Lom-bards had limited seamanship, and those fleeing them had sought the safety of Torcello and other islands in the lagoon.)

It is said that Narses, from his villa on the Bay, had given the Lombards the wink and nod to attack, so disgusted was he with the conduct of Justin II, Justinian I's nephew and successor. Under the leadership of Alboin, the Lombard federation established itself throughout the inland, if not the littoral, of an Italy still pros-trate from nearly twenty years of war between the Goths and the East. Exhausted by her victory in that contest, Byzantium could hold on to little more than Ravenna, Perugia, Rome, and Naples against the Lombard onslaught.

Alboin, the Lombard chieftain, was another of those macabre fairy-tale figures in which the Dark Ages abound. Before invading Italy, he'd launched his career by defeating a neighboring Germanic people, the Gepids, and murdering their king, Cunimund, whose skull Alboin fashioned into a drinking bowl, and whose daughter Rosamund he married. He wore the bowl on his belt, and is said to have forced Rosamund to drink from it too. That she intrigued against him comes as no surprise. Paulus Diaconus, an eighth-century Lombard historian, reports that "he who was most famous in war through the overthrow of many enemies perished by the scheme of one little woman."

The first Europe was Greece; the second, Rome; the third, Byzantium. The fourth Europe was this inexorable floodtide of strong-smelling tribesmen, nations from the back of beyond, hell-bent on conquest. It is they who made the Europe we know. One way to understand what happened at Naples in the early Middle Ages is to see the city as a bone of contention between the third Europe and the fourth. After the assassination of Alboin and, promptly, of his successor Cleph, the thirty-six Lombard dukes carved Italy into fiefdoms. Ensuing fratricidal wars among them dominated the rest of the seventh century. Diocesan cities were decimated; fertile lowlands were abandoned in favor of fortified hill towns; the old plantations gave way to subsistence farming; life throughout Campania grew increasingly precarious. Yet Naples, almost alone of those coastal places still under the nominal jurisdiction of Constantinople, remained independent of Lombard control. Its population swelled within fortifications rebuilt since Totila's destruction of the old wall, thousands from the hinterland having sought safety from Lombard depredations. Meanwhile the Neapolitan dukedom functioned more and more independently, paying lip service to Byzantium but going its own way politically and religiously. (The Eastern Empire was preoccupied in any case by the iconoclastic controversies that would dominate its internal life for a century.)

By the last quarter of the eighth century, however, there was a new juggernaut in Europe, the Franks, and the patchwork of bickering Lombard duchies would not survive them. In 774, Charlemagne, the great Frankish king, conquered all of Italy down to the southern border of the papal lands and declared himself master of the Lombards. Surviving Lombard redoubts were thenceforth in the South—at Benevento, Capua, and Salerno—boxing in the duchy of Naples. Evidently, relations with Byzantium were by then honored more in the breach than in the observance; early-ninth-century Neapolitan coinage shows the reigning duke or San Gennaro rather than any Byzantine *basileus.*

The two centuries after Charlemagne were about as dark as the two preceding him. Viking raiders from the north poured in, as did Magyars from the east, and Saracens from the south, ninth- and tenth-century protagonists in the essential Dark Age story: unwelcome visitors tearing the house down. The Saracens took Sicily from Byzantium in the course of the ninth century; it would be Muslim for two centuries before the Normans reclaimed it for Christendom. Charlemagne and his successors having enriched Rome's churches and monasteries, it was once again worthy of sacking, and in 846 the Arabs did so, despoiling even the tomb of Saint Peter in their search for gold and silver vessels and jeweled reliquaries. Travelers along the pilgrimage routes were routinely set upon, and

Saracen pirates made the Tyrrhenian and eastern Mediterranean extraordinarily dangerous waters. The great monasteries of San Vincenzo al Volturno and Monte Cassino were pillaged by Aghlabid Muslims from Sicily. We know that Naples, in the aftermath, felt compelled to treat with them, and permitted an Arab outpost at the foot of Vesuvius. Seeing that rival cities like Salerno and Capua were willing to employ Saracen mercenaries, Naples engaged freebooters too.

Thus Arab forces in ninth-century southern Italy were alternately feared and relied on. A tenth-century chronicler writes that when the Arabs near the Garigliano River "were at peace with the people of Salerno, they grievously afflicted the Neapolitans and the Capuans, and when they made peace with the Neapolitans, they attacked the cities of Salerno or Benevento." He adds that "they would invade the smaller towns and openly sell their Christian inhabitants." On the credit side, let us not neglect to mention that they brought to Italy—no small matter—lemons and oranges.

At Naples a single architectural monument survives whole from these years, the Pietrasanta bell tower. I like to have lunch in its shadow at an *osteria* called La Locanda del Grifo, the Inn of the Griffin. Any American in Italy sooner or later gets a craving for chicken. The many chicken butchers in the side streets would indicate that Italians like to prepare it at home. But order chicken in the eating establishments of Naples and you produce consternation. *Pollo, non ce l'ho,* you are told with a grimace. Somewhere in the mysterious depths of the Locanda, however, is always a chicken, because they know that coming down via dei Tribunali is an Anglo-Saxon palate getting hungry for it. (Among the staff here, my nickname is "Chicken." They don't think I'm in on the joke.) This afternoon I will have my favorite, chicken with peppers; the cook insinuates a hot one among the mild; delicious.

Pietrasanta bell tower dates, probably, from the turn of the twelfth century, but maybe earlier. Naples of the later dukedom must be inferred from it. We know that the Romanesque basilicas that sprang up were not inconsiderable. One bishop commissioned no fewer than five, one of which was here where I'm having lunch. Traces of it are still to be seen under the seventeenth-century church that now stands a little way off from the bell tower.

To get a better idea of what that basilica and the others were like, it is well worth making a short trip to Capua to see the exquisitely intact Sant'Angelo in Formis, one of the South's finest examples of Byzantine architecture and art in the early years of the second millennium. Sant'Angelo in Formis shows what the Naples of the dukedom would have looked like at its most splendid. Already in existence in the tenth century, between 1072 and 1087 the church and campanile were rebuilt and decorated as they remain today. The four Corinthian columns supporting the portico are, like much else in the design, salvaged from an ancient temple to Diana Tifatina that stood on the site. Inside, the pavements are mostly ancient, as are all of the fourteen columns marking out the central nave. The lectern of the central apse, a now headless eagle, is also presumably from the old temple. The frescoes, depicting scenes from both testaments, are of a blue-and-gold quickness and grace. Over here an archangel gently, regretfully, urges Adam and Eve from the garden, as if only asking them to leave a party that's over. And there, taking hold of Isaac by the hair, Abraham raises a long knife for the sacrifice, but an angel is at hand to say that religion will never again be about that. The sleeping disciples at Gethsemane snuggle together like puppies. A wide-eyed, attentive Jesus hangs calmly on the cross, looking satisfied to be there. All is delicate and witty, down to the feathery striped wings of the angels.

Is it too fanciful to imagine that in the church that once stood here at Naples angels of comparable quality spread their wings, done by perhaps the same hand as those at Capua? Many ingenious lovely things are gone. But there is this bell tower, inviting surmises about the city of a thousand years ago. No match, of course, for the high, massive, beautifully individual campaniles at the cathedrals of Gaeta and Amalfi, or at Santa Maria in Cosmedin in Rome, Sant'-Ambrogio in Milan, Pomposa abbey east of Ferrara, or San Zeno at Verona. Those towers embody Italian Romanesque at its most energetic.

But it is very pleasant to rest in the shade of this unheroic, undistinguished instance of the style. The low arch, through which the old *decumanus*, now via dei Tribunali, apparently ran, is embellished with *spoglie*—ancient funeral stones and pillars and architectural and sculptural elements, whatever was around. I have always wondered whether early medieval builders knew that this expedient, inherited from antiquity, made a wall or arch or pavement more beautiful. My little tower certainly benefits from it. A third of the way up, at one corner, is embedded a fragment of ancient sculpture, a griffin, namesake of the *osteria*. According to a legend universally believed in Naples, the area was once terrorized by a devil who would appear in the form of a pig. When a certain Bishop Pomponius had, through the intercession of the Madonna, succeeded in exorcising the demon, he decreed that a church in her honor should stand on the site. And when it was complete, the grateful populace adorned the summit of its bell tower with a little bronze porker. The church is gone, the pig is gone. The bell is gone, and about that disappearance I've been unable to identify even a legend. Weeds sprout from the mortar between the bricks. It's in terrible shape, Naples' only Romanesque monument, nearly a ruin, and it will simply collapse one day. *Il mattino* will blazon the item; northern papers will relegate it to page four. Won't be at all like the morning of July 14, 1902, when the old Venetian campanile of San Marco came crashing down. "The whole world mourned," says Jan Morris, and the refrain everywhere was *"Il Campanile è stato galantuomo"* ("The tower proved himself a gentleman"), for nobody but a tabby had died in the collapse. I hope that Pietrasanta, though shorter of stature and far less prepossessing, will show himself as great a gent when the day comes.

The hundreds of years of barbarian invasions created a new world in which it was much less clear who was barbarian. The Goths at Ravenna, for example, were representatives of much that was best in the East. As for the Lombards, it is clear on the artistic evidence at Pavia and elsewhere that they achieved a high civilization. The Frankish kings regarded themselves as successors to the old Western Empire.

Those at the ancient seats of power, Rome and Constantinople, acting on the high presumption of superior blood, could by contrast be as inhuman as any Saracen or Viking. In 1014, Eastern Emperor Basil II, after defeating the Bulgars at the battle of Kleidion, took fourteen thousand men prisoner and divided them into groups of a hundred. All but one of each group were blinded, the hundredth left with one eye so that he could lead his fellows home. Samuil, king of the Bulgars, is said to have dropped dead when he saw his returning troops.

"Crucible of Europe," Geoffrey Barraclough called the ninth and tenth centuries, since out of these very bleak times came the high medieval achievements of the twelfth and thirteenth: substantial increases in population throughout the continent; founding of new towns; large-scale clearance of forests for cultivation; dynamic new phases of Romanesque building and the emergence of Gothic; new forms of piety based on the teachings of Bernard of Clairvaux and Francis of Assisi; recovery of Greek and Latin texts and of Greek science augmented by Arab scholarship; establishment of the first universities. Those are the Middle Ages that people have been attracted to. But the unlovely and unloved ninth and tenth make a claim on my interest: Naples in that epoch faced adversaries on every side, and yet knew a cultural flowering under Duke Giovanni IV, who founded one of the great libraries of Europe and enriched the basilicas and monasteries. Was it he who caused my beloved bell tower of Pietrasanta to be built?

What Rome looked like at the outset of the ninth century we know, roughly. Naples is harder to visualize. A navigable river, the Sebeto, long since extinct, flowed down from Camaldoli to the port in Greek times, when Pizzofalcone had been home to the tomb of Parthenope. In the Roman era, an odeon and a smaller theater stood adjacent to each other, like those at Pompeii. Beyond the Roman wall, alongside the quay, were a stadium and a hippodrome; within the wall, a forum and basilicas, a *macellum*, or market, and municipal baths. All gone, with only traces surviving. But in the time of the

Longobardi and the Byzantines, most of these would still have been present, in whatever state of disuse and decay.

Friends arriving fresh from the glorious sights of Rome complain that at Naples there is no Colosseum, no Forum, no Baths of Caracalla or Markets of Trajan, no Palatine Hill. I always try to convince them that Naples is, even more profoundly than Rome, a story of all the four Europes. Look at this grid of streets, I say, *decumani* running east to west, *cardines* north to south, just as the Greeks laid them out two and a half millennia ago. I've even swatted up suitable lines from Marlowe's *Doctor Faustus*:

> *Then up to Naples, rich Campania,*
> *Whose buildings fair and gorgeous to the eye,*
> *The streets straight forth, and pav'd with finest brick,*
> *Quarter the town in four equivalents.*

But Naples is just too shaggy a tale to tell. Even the politest people glaze over somewhere between Odoacer and Bishop Pomponius, and I am learning, at the tender age of fifty-nine, not to bore friends with things of interest only to me. At least I like to think so.

THREE

The Very True Truths

*Since our youth, before assuming the burden of rule, we have
sought knowledge, loved its beauty, and breathed tirelessly
the smell of its perfumes.*

—Emperor Frederick II of Hohenstaufen, in a letter
to the faculty of the University of Bologna

S uppose you could convene the most humane and liber-
ating thinkers of the eighteenth and nineteenth centuries—the
philosophes, Hume, Kant, Tocqueville, Mill, Herzen—and tell them
about the staggering millions who would be sacrificed in the twentieth century to this or that inhuman ideology? They would not believe
you. Such a reversion to barbarism could not possibly be what the
future held. And what if you were to impart the very bad twenty-
first-century news: that atavistic religious ideologies are now to have
their day? They would not believe you. The way out of religious
lunacy had been so hard-won, from the wars of religion culminating
in the Thirty Years' War, through the gradual development of toleration, the growth of secular learning and scientific advancement, the
increasing confinement of religious emotions to the private sphere.

What the aforementioned minds had in common was their certainty
that secularism was the intellectual and social goal. The honor roll
is expandable as you like, of course; all the articulate enemies of sec-
tarianism and superstition belong there. I want to add the name of a
philosopher who might have understood the historical ghastliness as
well as any of those more famous figures: Charles Renouvier, faded
though his reputation is. Look to this forgotten Frenchman if you
want to know where pragmatism, America's leading philosophical
idea, came from. When William James writes, in 1907, "Truth *happens* to an idea. It *becomes* true, is *made* true by events," he is echoing
his great teacher Renouvier, who had saved James from mental sick-
ness with the proposition that we know ourselves free in a universe
of pure contingency, orphaned of its old consoling theistic myths,
because we may entertain the thoughts we choose instead of enter-
taining others. Having absorbed this from Renouvier's second series
of *Essais* in 1870, James confided to his diary: "I will assume for the
present—until next year—that it is no illusion. My first act of free
will shall be to believe in free will." Renouvier's whole project was to
release us from every check on our sense of the *liberum arbitrium*,
whether it be tragic Fate or Christian Providence or "the cunning
of history" or dialectical materialism or any other ism purporting to
define us and foretell our future. His philosophical "novel" *Uchronie*, subtitled *L'utopie dans l'histoire: Esquisse historique apocryphe
du développement de la civilisation européenne tel qu'il n'a pas été,
tel qu'il aurait pu être* (Utopia in History: Sketch of an Apocryphal
History of the Development of European Civilization As It Was Not
but Might Have Been), still makes a powerful impact with its alternative narrative of Rome, positing a more appealing way things might

have come out. As a utopia is a place that neither was, nor is, nor will be, a uchronia is a *time* that was not, a counterhistory.

The library copy of Renouvier's *Uchronie* on my desk, dating from the 1870s when first it appeared, had not left its shelf since before I was born. To read an exciting and very forgotten book is one of the great experiences. To encounter the figures of Roman history saying and doing what they emphatically did not say or do is an exhilaration. Professional historians shun alternative scenarios, admonish us that history does not reveal its alternatives and that it is idle to spin counterhistories. But spin them we do, especially those of us who, with Renouvier, see only contingency where others have posited laws of historical development. *Uchronie* bases itself on the beguiling premise that Christianity might have failed to conquer Europe, been beaten back, remained Oriental, then entered Europe belatedly as one religion among others, Greco-Roman, Jewish, Mithraic, Pythagorean, et cetera. Religion might have evolved pacifically in Europe. Would it were so, says every word of Renouvier's counterhistory; how much Europe could have been spared. The counterhistory in his book is in fact a forbidden document handed down from generation to generation in an ostensibly pious Catholic family. A blasphemous alternative history of Rome, written by a sixteenth-century priest later burned at the stake for his secret view that we would all have been better-off without Christ's triumph, it is this family's hidden and dangerous patrimony. The text has magical properties: to read it is to be disabused forever of the baleful Christian spell under which Europe was laid.

Western Europe is nowadays post-Christian. The churches, Catholic and Protestant alike, stand more or less empty in Germany,

France, England. In the great cities of northern Italy it is no different. Bologna, so chic and gastronomical, is no place for the Good News. The good news there is a new *bottega* or *enoteca*. Even here in Naples, where the standard of living is half that of Bologna, the young have a healthy disrespect for the Roman Catholic faith, however proudly they may look back on the superstitious extremes their great-grandparents went to. Young *napoletani* studying for the priesthood tend to be regarded by their peers as mental and moral defectives, which not a few are.

And yet—sad story we know too well—this increasing confinement of Christianity in Europe coexists with evangelical big business and big political clout in the United States. (It would be foolhardy to believe that this reached its high-water mark in the George W. Bush years and is now ebbing. One knows one's native land better than that.) And both Roman Catholicism and evangelical Christianity are growth industries in sub-Saharan Africa. The young friars and nuns you see hurrying through the streets of Naples are likely as not Africans resident in one or another of the city's monasteries, as are many of those in the closed orders.

I think that Renouvier, who took the measure of religious compulsion as no one else had—rather than just mocking it or declaring it superannuated—might well have understood the world-historical trouble we're in. Shortly before his death in 1903, amid other people's high hopes for the new century, Renouvier said he saw a dark night ahead. The modern nightmare of world wars and vast social cleansings did come. Could Renouvier stand with us 135 years later, would his grounds for pessimism be fewer or more? What will the species still have to undergo? But "have to undergo" is an illicit phrase, says Renouvier. No historical outcomes are preordained, nothing is bound to occur. I will assume for the present—until tomorrow morning—that this is no illusion.

On that thought, I close my notebook and head off for a look at the bare traces of Norman times here. Sicily not Naples is where to go to see what the leading eleventh- and twelfth-century vanquishers achieved: the cathedrals at Cefalù and Monreale, the Palazzo dei Normanni and Cappella Palatina at Palermo with their incomparable hybridization of Arab, Byzantine, and Norman styles. (Augustus Hare called the Cappella Palatina "an ecclesiastical *coup d'oeil* unequalled in Italy.") Having wrested Sicily from two hundred years of tolerant, civilized Arab rule, Norman kings employed the Arabo-Byzantine architects and craftsmen who had been in place for generations. The taste these blond beasts brought with them underwent profound changes, as inevitably happens when a ruder people conquers a more refined one.

Who were they, the invading Normans? Vikings who had settled in the north of France at the turn of the tenth century. Within a century and a half they were making incontrovertible history, conquering Anglo-Saxons to the north and Saracens, Longobardi, and Byzantines to the south (much as another breed of Viking, the Rus', had done in the region around Kiev two centuries earlier). But whereas William the Conqueror's work was accomplished in a single famous battle, the Normans in the South were soldiers of fortune offering themselves to whichever faction paid best, and coming only in the course of decades to subdue their employers and make themselves masters of what was thenceforth called Regnum Siciliae, the Kingdom of Sicily, meaning the island as well as all of the Mezzogiorno. Naples was among the last citadels to fall to them: 1139 is late in the day. A nineteenth-century statue of Roger II in a niche of the façade of Palazzo Reale shows him, ferocious in chain mail, taking the measure of Parthenope, this prize that had for so long eluded him. The blood that flowed in Roger was Norse: Normans, Northmen, Norsemen—"Scandinavian pirates," Gibbon bluntly, accurately, called them. They settled on the northern shore of France and, with their assimilative gifts, became Christian and Romance-speaking. What they brought with them seems to have been little more than a confident illiteracy joined to fantastic extremes of cruelty—recreational cutting off of ears and genitals and gouging out of eyes. They seem also to have been excessively fond of pilgrimages; it was on the return from one of these in 1016 that a band of them was invited into the service of an embattled Apulian prince. They declined, but spread word through Normandy that there were both money and renown to be earned in the strife-torn realms south of Rome.

By 1030, one soldier of fortune, Rainulf, had taken as reward for his services the town of Aversa, very near to Naples. Word of his initial success seems to have made the journey irresistible to penniless young knights back in the towns of Normandy. From Coutances came the sons of Tancred de Hauteville: William Iron-Arm, who was count of Apulia by 1042; Drogo and Humphrey, his younger brothers and successors to the title; and, from Tancred's second marriage, Robert Guiscard and Roger, his much younger brother, who, before he was done, had dislodged the Saracens from Sicily and established a dynasty there. Roger II, who gazes out on piazza del Plebiscito from his niche, was that Roger's son. On the evidence of what they produced, in architecture and in poetry, Italy decisively changed them, as it changed Lombards and Goths, indeed has changed every culture that made serious contact with it, however brutally, from the barbarian invasions to the present. Roger II, for example, had starved two-thirds of Naples to death inside its fortified walls before the city finally fell to him. And yet, in the long term, it was the Normans' susceptibility to cultural influences flowing to them from the conquered that proved most decisive.

The great Norman monuments, as I say, are in Palermo, Monreale, Cefalù; and in Puglia, whose Castel del Monte adorns the one-penny euro. At Naples there is little left to see. As I wrestle with these blond-haired shadows in a sepulchral reading room of the Biblioteca Nazionale one afternoon, I win the compassion of a young woman sitting opposite. Observing my despair over some dull book about the *normanni*, or perhaps some marvelous book too difficult for me—I don't remember which—she passes a note my way: "May I speak with you, about an American matter?" This can't be good. I follow her into the corridor. She proposes a walk in the garden. "You *are* American?" I nod. Within Palazzo Reale, where the library is housed, is a beautiful palm-shaded square. It is a place for the young. Here you see love start up and flourish and peter out. In good weather I've taken to snacking on the grass, and one afternoon watched all three phases unfold in the shade of different trees. The young woman introduces herself as Gabriella. We seat ourselves on the lawn. She speaks English well, so I stow my feeble Italian. She says she's as downhearted about her researches as I appear to be about mine. Says she's writing an essay on William Faulkner. On *Absalom, Absalom!* no less. "Do you happen to have read it?"

"You bet."

"Excuse me?"

"I have, yes. A favorite author of mine."

"Above Ernest Hemingway?"

"They're so different. But yes, if forced to choose, I'd go with Faulkner."

"Harder to *read* than Ernest Hemingway, however."

"You bet."

"Excuse me?"

"Yes, harder." How, I wonder, is she coping with *Absalom, Absalom!* if "You bet" confuses her? Gabriella's English is decidedly *English*. She spent a year in London, I learn later. Was it there she picked up the bluestocking manner? And her preference for being called "Gabby"? She wears a sloppy sweater (for which the day is too warm), a badly hemmed skirt, a pair of off-kilter eyeglasses, and lumpy-looking shoes. And how this girl can *smoke!* She's blue from it. But before the shadows have time to lengthen or the day to grow cool, I am taking instruction from her in my native literature.

"This *Absalom, Absalom!* is preposterously hard."

"Hard books are an American speciality, Gabby. Have you heard of *The Golden Bowl* by Henry James? Or the *Collected Poems* of Wallace Stevens? Or *Gravity's Rainbow*?"

"And why do you think Americans write such things?"

"The women don't, as a rule. It's some kind of apocalyptic yearning, and it's mostly male. Faulkner says he's trying to get it all in between one capital and one full stop. The more you read about him, the less accountable his great books are. I mean, how did a thing like *Absalom*, as clear-cut a work of genius as any, come to be? He's got funny little deficiencies, you know. Doesn't get the difference between 'like' and 'as.' Thinks 'infer' and 'imply' are synonyms. But in that ocean of words, who cares?" Against all the odds, I'd found somebody in Naples I could talk to about the things I know best, my birthright, as it were, sacred to me, unbartered for any mess of pottage.

She produces from her satchel a dog-eared copy of *Absalom*. "Take the last sentence: '*I don't hate it* he thought, panting in the cold air, the iron New England dark; *I don't. I don't! I don't hate it! I don't hate it!*'"

"As a Neapolitan, you'll be able to work that out for yourself. It's the South he's telling himself he doesn't hate."

"I do, indeed, tell myself, 'I don't hate Naples, I don't hate it, I don't, I don't.'"

"The political culture of the United States is dominated by what Faulkner called Snopeses, proudly ignorant, proudly small. Some days, observing their knaveries, I say to myself, 'I don't hate the United States, I don't, I don't.' The deeper, the real patriotism is in being torn, I think. It's taking account of all your country has perpetrated, for good and for ill. We've done impressively bad things on the world stage in my lifetime, always professing the highest motives. Has any empire ever had finer-sounding reasons for the misbegotten wars it has waged?"

"But your president, he is no Snopes."

"Obama? An intellectual. An anti-Snopes. Which is why in Snopesland he's so despised. I mean, murderously despised. For being reflective, large-spirited, erudite. These are unforgivable traits. And to add to the outrage, he is of mixed race."

She lights another cigarette. Italy went *non fumatori* some years back, but Neapolitan smokers are not over the shock. Sidewalks and public squares teem with them, puffing for all they're worth. "Have you such nonsense in America as this ban?"

"New York and Los Angeles are *non fumatori*. Chicago, too. It's a municipal matter. But go ahead." Her funeral. "Gabriella, some people think reading Faulkner is like eating a rug. Most, really. I'm impressed that you can do it."

"Oh, I don't understand everything. What, for example, is a 'scuppernong arbor'? What is 'Manassas'? What is 'the old imbecile stability of the articulated mud'?"

"Manassas was a battle. With those other two you're on your own."

"What I like is to let the sentences wash over me. It makes me feel I'm turning into someone else."

"Well, that is certainly my own view of reading, or of travel, or of loving, for that matter. But I think your professor expects you to find out rather than just metamorphose. Unless he's a greater romantic even than you and me."

"He is a lesser romantic than you and me." And presto, we are fast friends.

"One day, when America's deeds are done and the glory finished and the whole story gets sifted by some Gibbon of the remote future, among the very best American things will probably be that far-seeing book in your lap. What's it finally about, do you think? Imagine those sentences you love as iron filings in a dish. What's the magnet under the dish that gives them the particular shape they stand up in?"

"Is this how you think of books?"

"Seems a good-enough metaphor for the relation of language to theme, yes."

"Don't you mean form to content?"

"No, those two words are troublemakers. Language to theme."

"All right, then. I would say the theme is—empire. The rise and fall of the Sutpens. From the original humiliation that drives Thomas Sutpen's ambition, that he was turned away from the front door of a villa in the state of Tidewater—"

"Virginia. The Tidewater's the southeastern part of it. Mansion, not villa."

"—from the door of a mansion in the state of Virginia, told by a slave to go to the back door. On to how he bought a hundred acres of Yoknapatawpha land from"—here she consults her notes—"Chief Ikkemotubbe—"

"You're good, Gabby! And the building of the great plantation house and marriage to the suitable young woman and siring of children and making his empire safe from all adversity, all of it according to a scheme he'd formed when he had nothing but youth and rage and innocence to guide him—"

"Beniamino, you *sound* like Faulkner!" She takes up the book and reads: " 'He was unaware that his flowering was a forced blooming too and that while he was still playing the scene to the audience, behind him Fate, destiny, retribution, irony—the stage manager, call him what you will—was already striking the set and dragging on the synthetic and spurious shadows and shapes of the next one.' But tell me, was there an actual family he based all that on? Is it a true story?"

"It's truer than true, it's literature. To think that a humiliated and beleaguered Mississippian foresaw the whole American story. Yes, that seems to me what the book's really about—Fate, or Nemesis, or whatever you want to call it picking out the time and place and way to whipsaw you. It's what I love about this city of yours, you know. That it's been whipsawed every which way for more than two and a half millennia. I'm writing about Naples, you're writing about Yoknapatawpha. Each is a place where too much has happened, where the blood is on the ground and the glory has inexorably passed away into a storied past and the present is a diminished thing and the future lies open, as every future does, to blind chance. Turns out we're writing about the same thing, Gabby."

"Let's have a glass of something on that. At the Gambrinus?"

"A glass of bourbon, in honor of You Know Who." We pull together our belongings and head that way.

Caffè Gambrinus is sacred ground, like the Flore in Paris, the Central in Vienna, the Pedrocchi in Padua, the Quatre Gats in Barcelona. Founded in 1860, the year of national unification, it's been the haunt of Naples' most brilliant and creative personalities. Figures of pan-European importance have turned up too: Maupassant, Oscar Wilde. The Gambrinus anchors one side of piazza Trieste e Trento, its windows enticing at dusk with their lambent glow and glimpses of ardent conversation. Enter and you're in an over-

Caffè Gambrinus, 1936

heated jewel box. A selection of phantasmagorical cakes and tarts grabs the eye. We seat ourselves among people chatting, eating, reading newspapers on wooden rods. Ahead of drinks, Gabby orders a slice of *torta mocha*. I get the lemon thing.

"I'm curious. Were your family here during the war?"

"Mamma is from Salerno. But Babbo grew up right here. He doesn't speak about the bombings, the hunger, the Germans, the things he saw as a child. He has only one or two memories of his own father, who died in the Abyssinian War. His mother, my Nonna Maria, kept a portrait of her dead husband in full military dress above the mantel of her flat in via Chiaia, and fresh flowers around the frame. She was very elderly by the time I knew her, one of those shapeless women dressed in black. I remember how *medicinale*—what is the word in English?"

"The same."

"—how medicinal the flat smelled. She'd been a widow for so many years. Silent, unsmiling old lady. No tenderness. Nineteen thirty-five had done for her."

I like the "done for," a turn she must have picked up in England. I like everything about this formidably intelligent young woman. She asks me why I'm so often in the National Library. I tell about my researches, if that's not too pretentious a word for what I've been doing. ("Browsing" would be more accurate.) I tell her that the good kings interest me in a world where most have been so bad. Among medieval European sovereigns, there is one I'd like to have known: Frederick II of Hohenstaufen, thirteenth-century founder of the University of Naples. His grandfathers were Roger II on his mother's side and Frederick Barbarossa on his father's. In his veins the blood royal of the Swabian kings commingled with that of the Norman Hautevilles. As a child he was Puer Siciliae, the boy of Sicily, and grew up wild in the quasi-Oriental streets and souks of Palermo. In maturity, he was Holy Roman Emperor and Stupor Mundi, the wonder of the world. That he survived to manhood at all is miraculous. The brutalities his Hohenstaufen father, Henry VI, had visited on Sicily and the southern mainland gave grounds for no end of loathing. In Palermo, on the Feast of Saint Stephen,

1194—on the very day, in fact, of Frederick's birth in far-off Jesi, in the Marches—Henry had celebrated his own coronation by blinding and castrating the eight-year-old Norman heir whose claims he'd outflanked; he had hundreds of the Sicilian aristocracy burned alive, and ordered the corpse of the previous king, Tancred, pulled from his grave so that the body could be decapitated in full view of the Palermitan populace.

Such was the Feast of Stephen that Henry's son had to live down. As a learning-loving man of twenty-six (he knew no fewer than six languages), having by right of succession to his mother been crowned king of Sicily, Frederick was by right of succession to his father crowned Holy Roman Emperor. More Renaissance prince or eighteenth-century enlightened despot than medieval suzerain, he called to his court Leonardo Fibonacci, the scientist most responsible for the spread of Arabic numerals in the West, as well as the great medieval scholar Michael Scot of Toledo, who translated Aristotle and Arabic works into Latin. Frederick's court prominently included troubadour poets from Provence and a school of Sicilian poets who, inspired by the troubadours, founded the earliest tradition of vernacular poetry in Italy. Frederick's code of law, the Liber Augustalis, set the standard for more humane lawmaking and remained the basis for southern Italian law well into the nineteenth century. He meant to rival the very greatest of the Roman emperors, including Augustus and the good Antonines, and so he did.

A religious doubter by temperament, Frederick seems to have denounced each of the Abrahamic religions in turn, not sparing Christianity, and also to have earnestly studied them. His toleration of Muslims and Jews throughout the South produced a cosmopolitanism that would not be known again till modern times. He commissioned for himself a coronation cloak ornamented at the border—doubtless to the amazement of Pope Innocent II and all others who saw it—with camels and tigers and an Arabic benediction. (The cloak may be seen today in the Schatzkammer of Vienna's Kunsthistorisches Museum.) When in 1229 he all-but-bloodlessly retook Jerusalem, he complained at the cessation of the muezzins' call to prayer, since it was to hear this, he said, that he'd come. His passion for mathematics and the natural sciences had understandably led him to honor the culture of Islam, which he recognized as intellectually and aesthetically in advance of the West. He seems to have made a careful study of the Dome of the Rock and modeled his octagonal Apulian hunting lodge, Castel del Monte, after it. As for the Jews, they enjoyed in Naples and in the other cities of Frederick's kingdom a golden age. Arrivals from Spain and Provence, by and large, they were neither ghettoized nor confined to moneylending. And while Frederick's laws required that Jews wear a distinguishing blue-gray linen cloak, among the learned doctors called to his court were Jehuda ben Salomon Cohen of Toledo, philosopher, astronomer, and mathematician; Moses ben Salomon of Salerno, translator and exegete of Maimonides' *Guide for the Perplexed*; and Jacob Anatoli of Marseille, leading Talmudist and astronomer of the day, who described Frederick as "a lover of learning who was my patron. May God grant him his blessing to the end that he may be elevated above all kings, and may the Messiah come during his reign!"

Gabby has ordered a Cinzano with soda and I ask for whiskey. The waiter brings the bottle of Jack Daniel's, which he displays as if it were a bottle of wine. I always get a bang out of this gesture. We lift glasses and I teach her my grandfather's toast, "Happy Days!"

(A memory floods back unbidden: How he raised a glass and said it, tears coming down his face, after my grandmother's funeral.)

The end of the Hohenstaufen in Italy and Sicily makes a pitiful tale. Would that Frederick could have lived forever. (In Dante he does, like every soul. Frederick's specific fate is to be roasted with Epicureans in the sixth circle of Hell.) At the battle of Benevento (1266), his natural son Manfred was defeated and slain by Charles I of Anjou, whom Pope Urban IV had invited to conquer the South. Two years later, having secured his conquest at the battle of Tagliacozzo, Charles brought the defeated young grandson of Frederick, sixteen-year-old Conradin, to piazza Mercato and there had the boy and his retinue beheaded, an event that would for generations warm the hearts of papal loyalists (Guelfs) and inspire horror in those favoring Holy Roman Imperial prerogatives (Ghibellines). "Oh, Mother, what a grief this day brings you!" the boy cried out as he bent to the block. Upon this crime, and in the teeth of popular rage and hatred, the Angevins established themselves. Eighteen years after Frederick's death, the Hohenstaufen were thus extinguished.

Conradin's body reposes behind the high altar of the Church of Santa Maria del Carmine Maggiore in Naples under a stone marked simply *R. C. C.* (*Regis Corradini Corpus*). Missing for nearly four hundred years, the remains came to light in the seventeenth century when workmen digging in piazza Mercato inadvertently struck a lead-lined casket, similarly marked *R. C. C.* Within were the skeleton and severed skull, as well as Conradin's sword and other attributes. He was the heart's cry for centuries here.

Sprung from the loins of conquerors, he came to stand in Angevin, Aragonese, Spanish, and Bourbon times for resistance and forlorn hope, a child martyr to the cause of Neapolitan independence.

A spontaneous revolt fourteen years into Charles I's reign—the so-called Sicilian Vespers—would deprive him of Sicily, which passed into Aragonese hands. Out of this "amputation," as Benedetto Croce calls it, Naples as we know it began to grow. With Palermo forfeit, Naples became capital of the now truncated kingdom. Among architectural achievements of this time are a number of churches in the distinctive Neapolitan take on French Gothic. Masterpieces of a harsh beauty not universally admired, they mean more to me than other surviving structures here. Primo Levi says: "There have been centuries in which 'beauty' was identified with adornment, the superimposed, the frills; but it is probable that they were deviant epochs and that the true beauty, in which every century recognizes itself, is found in upright stones, ships' hulls, the blade of an ax, the wing of a plane." Levi's words provide the best gloss on Santa Chiara, Sant'Eligio Maggiore, San Lorenzo Maggiore, Santa Maria Incoronata, or San Pietro a Majella, divested now of the Baroque adornments that used to encase them: not the filigree of Gothic but the bare bones, a Gothic for those with the natural preference for Romanesque. (At least until some new taste—for Baroque, Rococo, Neoclassicism, or the Modern—captures you.) There was never here the stained glass on which northern Europe prided itself. Clear panes in leaded mullions sufficed. Nor is the sublime verticality of Chartres or Amiens to be found; truss-beam ceilings over large, open, boxlike sanctuaries were the rule. When Santa Chiara was nearly complete, Robert the Wise brought his son Charles, duke of Calabria, to see it. The young man, presumably

imbued with French tastes, loathed what he saw, and said that the
vast unpillared nave put him in mind of a stable, the side chapels
of horse stalls. The king's response was formal and curt: *"Piaccia
a Dio, o mio figliuolo, che non siete il primo a mangiare in questa
scuderia"* ("May it please God, my son, that you not be first to eat in
this stable"). History records no retort of son to father; I doubt there
could have been one.

The religious order at Santa Chiara was Franciscan, and in
keeping with the Franciscan rule, walls were flat and frescoed. The
visual ideal was a continuous storytelling in images. Everywhere
the faithful looked should be chapter and verse of the Gospels and
the lives of the saints. But what is whole at the Arena Chapel in
Padua or Santa Maria Novella in Florence or (mostly, despite damage from the 1997 earthquake) San Francesco in Assisi is ruined or
lost in Naples. What remains has a fragmentary beauty that would
have been incomprehensible to the late-thirteenth- and fourteenth-
century masters to whom this great artistic revolution is owed;

Cappella Minutolo, Duomo

would have been incomprehensible to all
tastes before the modern. Take, for example,
Cappella Minutolo in the Duomo. If forced
to declare one Neapolitan place more beautiful than all others, I would choose this chapel,
originally freestanding, incorporated from the
fourteenth century into the expanding matrix
of the cathedral. You may stare in through
the gates but not enter. My application to the
Soprintendenza for permission has vanished
into the void each time I've sent it. Flourish
my credentials as I like, no response. Earlier

travelers did not have these gates to contend with. Hare describes walking in at publicly appointed hours. I think the fragile Cosmati pavement, dating from the end of the thirteenth century, must be what has closed the place down.

Gabby takes me one morning to visit a hidden supremacy of this Neapolitan Gothic, the deconsecrated church of Santa Maria Incoronata. King Robert's granddaughter Giovanna I, who ruled from 1343 to 1381, married Luigi, prince of Taranto, in 1347, at the time of the Black Death; it was the second of her four marriages. To memorialize her coronation she built Santa Maria Incoronata, incorporating the earlier church that stood there, and commissioned a fresco cycle of the Seven Sacraments. Gabby points out the marriage panel, Giovanna in royal raiment and her bridegroom with long red hair and beard and crowned with laurel. A violinist plays as courtiers dance. These frescoes used to be attributed to Giotto, though this can't be; the wedding took place ten years after his death. They are by Giotto's preeminent follower in Naples, Roberto d'Oderisio.

"*Poverina,*" says Gabby. "After thirty-eight years as queen, Giovanna's cousin Carlo Durazzo usurped the kingdom and sent her into exile in Basilicata, where his henchmen smothered her in a feather bed. She gets little respect from the historians. But I like her."

"You know, I've got this need," I explain to Gabby over coffee one morning, "to single out the Jewish story. One point five billion Muslims, two point one million Christians, nine hundred million Hindus, four hundred million Buddhists. As against fourteen million Jews. But they're my lens on everything."

"The Jews are a small story here in Naples. The Angevins and the Spanish saw to that throughout the South. But between them came, for half a century, the Aragonese. The Jews did well here under them. In fact, Naples near the end of the fifteenth century may have been briefly as Jewish as, say, Vienna at the start of the twentieth."

I give her a look. Why settle for Vienna? Go for broke. Tell me Naples was as Jewish as Warsaw or Odessa. I am learning that historical accuracy is not Gabriella's strong suit.

"Hard to imagine, but they say it's so. It was during our little Renaissance. Second half of the Quattrocento. Then came two centuries of the dreadful Spanish, whose blood flows in all our veins. In modern times some Jews finally did come back. Under the Bourbons. When they discovered their coffers were empty, a Rothschild was invited down. You have visited our little synagogue in vico Santa Maria a Cappella Vecchia?"

"Our little synagogue": the Neapolitan not the Jewish "our," and I hear in it the patriotism of Naples, wounded, rueful, sure of its ground. I have indeed, one Saturday morning, visited their little synagogue. A plaque to the right of the doorway commemorates Neapolitan victims of the Holocaust. Of the 7,500 Italian Jews who perished in the camps, a scant fourteen were from Naples. Because of the Reich's hasty retreat in late September 1943, the Nazis had no opportunity to deport the city's small Jewish population. These fourteen were Neapolitans seized away from home, either in Rome or in other Italian cities where the Germans were carrying out aggressive roundups in the autumn of 1943 and winter of 1944. The plaque names the fourteen, among them thirteen-month-old Paolo Amedeo Procaccia, murdered with his father, Aldo, and mother, Milena, at Auschwitz on February 6, 1944. The synagogue nowadays serves a community of no more than two or three hundred Jews. The rite is Sephardic, of course, the look and feel exactly what you find in the synagogues of Venice or Ferrara or Rome, only miniaturized. The "rabbi," stroking a downy young beard, hastened to tell me he was still at seminary. On the walls I saw, among the nineteenth-century names, TAYLOR (and also TAJLOR), Jews evidently in the entourage of Carl Rothschild.

"They are surely your relatives," says Gabby when I report on this. "I knew you were Neapolitan, Beniamino. I knew it all along."

"Not possibly. My great-grandfather Taylor was born Trashensky in Russian Poland. He became Taylor at Galveston, Texas, not Liverpool or Portsmouth. And no sooner than 1907."

"But I choose to believe that they are your forebears. It makes sense that they should be. It explains you. The *verissima verità*, the very true truth, is that they are your forebears."

"Gabriella, those Taylors on the synagogue wall are no kin of mine." I pay the check and we hasten to San Giovanni a Carbonara Vecchia. Gabby says that she has stupendous things to show me there.

"Will you consent to be blindfolded?"

"Don't be ridiculous."

"I want you to see things in their proper order." When we reach the portal she takes a scarf from her satchel and ties it around my head.

"This thing stinks of cigarettes, Gabby."

"It's only for a minute." She leads me in. Through the scarf I get intimations. Now she removes it and I am in a smallish high-ceilinged room filled by a dazzling, many-layered funeral monument. "This is the tomb of King Ladislao, son and successor of Carlo Durazzo. His

Funeral monument of King Ladislao Durazzo, San Giovanni a Carbonara Vecchia

death in 1414 is unique in the annals of regicide. Ladislao was impossible to poison, as the royal tasters sampled everything before he ate. His mistress was an apothecary's daughter from Perugia. Ladislao's enemies, figuring out the one dish his tasters would not sample before him, convinced this girl, before making love with the king, to anoint her genitals with what they told her was an aphrodisiacal unguent, but was in fact a poison."

And what became of the apothecary's daughter, I'd like to know. She must have died too, and first. Ladislao's epitaph makes no reference to his outlandish death, content to say: "Unrighteous death, alas, is ever unexpected in the affairs of men. / Just as the magnanimous king bathes the world in hope, / Lo, he dies: the noble king was roofed over by this stone, / While his soul, single and free, sought starry Olympus."

The masterpiece of one Andrea di Onofrio (also called Ciccione), Ladislao's tomb stands eighteen meters tall, nearly the full height of the church. The first level is dominated by four allegorical caryatids—Justice, Prudence, Temperance, Fortitude—who carry the whole structure and frame a gate. At the next level, the king and his mother are surrounded by Faith, Charity, Loyalty, and Hope. The third level has angels drawing aside an arras to reveal the sarcophagus in which the king's body lies. And surmounting the whole is Ladislao on horseback, sword raised. We pass through the gate of the tomb. What we enter is an octagonal chapel, completely frescoed. More of the Neapolitan school of Giotto, it looks like. Gabby confirms my guess. Before us is the sepulchre (also attributed by some to Andrea di Onofrio) of Ser Gianni Caracciolo, as he's colloquially known, lusted after by Ladislao's sister and successor, Giovanna II.

"The queen learned by devious means that Ser Gianni's greatest fear was rats. She arranged for a servant to unleash a cage of them in a hallway as he was passing. Desperate to get away from the rats, he tried every door, but only that of the queen's bedchamber was unlocked. And that's how he became her lover."

"Gabby, that story, too, has something rum about it. I mean, it doesn't make a lot of sense."

"These are the legends," she says. "The very true truths." And she puts a finger to my lips.

On the way home I pass Castel Nuovo, beheld with new eyes. Ladislao's funeral monument is a middle term, I see now, between the old Gothic and the Aragonese Renaissance epitomized in the Triumphal Arch of Alfonso the Magnanimous between the two turrets of the entry. Like Angevin tombs, the Arch is built up of scenes superimposed one atop another, iconographies in vertical sequence. But where Ladislao's tomb at San Giovanni is static, the Arch shows a procession passing. Alphonsus Triumphator rides in glory through the

Detail of Triumphal Arch at Castel Nuovo

streets of conquered Naples. (A Roman-style triumph had in fact been celebrated for him in 1443, upon his conquest of the kingdom.) Designed by Francesco Laurana and others, the Arch must have astonished Neapolitans' eyes in the fifteenth century, for nothing else in their civic or religious life resembled it. Thus began the "little Renaissance" of Naples.

In the Church of Santa Maria di Monteoliveto, later also called Sant'Anna dei Lombardi, it reached its culmination. Though gravely damaged in the Second World War, this complex has now been splendidly restored. Four of the church's chapels remain as they were when Alfonso II of Naples, grandson of the Magnanimous, caused Monteoliveto to be expanded as a royal pantheon, the finest expression of his enlightened reign. The cloister is nowadays in use by the Carabinieri, and no display of credentials gets you past them for a look. Still, there are rewards enough. The Piccolomini Chapel, adjacent to the western vestibule, contains the ravishing sepulchre of Alfonso II's half sister, Maria of Aragon, whose epitaph translates thus: "You who read these words, do so in a low voice lest you wake the sleeper. Mary of Aragon, a child of King Ferdinand, is enclosed within. She married the stalwart duke of Malfi, Antonio Piccolomini, to whom she left three daughters as a witness of their mutual love. One can believe she is sleeping, for she little deserved to die."

The tomb was begun by the Florentine Antonio Rossellino and completed by Benedetto da Maiano. Benedetto was the leading Italian sculptor in marble between Donatello and Michelangelo. In the architecturally identical Terranova Chapel, on the other side of the narthex at Monteoliveto, is his *Annunciation*, the most beautiful

The Annunciation *by Benedetto da Maiano, Terranova Chapel, Church of Santa Maria di Monteoliveto*

bas-relief in Naples. The Archangel Gabriel, having presented the (now lost) lily signifying Mary's election, crosses his hands and gazes at her in adoration. Mary clasps her left breast with her right hand and reaches for her womb with the left, the hand in which she still holds the Scripture she was reading when Gabriel surprised her. The impregnating dove of the Holy Ghost, dispatched from the triune figure of the godhead in the upper left corner, rides a diagonal that points to her womb. Angel and woman stand beneath a forced perspective of coffered arches giving onto a walled garden—the *hortus conclusus* of the Song of Songs, for medieval Christians the allegorical emblem of the purity of the Mother of God: *"Hortus conclusus soror mea, sponsa, hortus conclusus, fons signatus"* ("A garden inclosed is my sister, my spouse; a spring shut up, a garden sealed"). Christianity locates the Old Testament *figura*, or prefiguration, of Christ's immaculate conception in the Song of Songs: "Thou art all fair, my love, there is no spot in thee." Benedetto has represented the moment of highest drama, just as the fullness of the Virgin's appointment with destiny dawns on her. Shouldering infinite mystery, the young woman becomes something more—becomes the *mater dolorosa*, too, seeing all the way to Golgotha.

These meticulous, exquisite, Florentine-inspired marble figures of the Piccolomini and Terranova chapels have their Renaissance

The Lamentation *by Guido Mazzoni,*
Church of Santa Maria di Monteoliveto

opposite in the slightly later sculpture of Monteoliveto's large south chapel. There you come with a start upon the life-size *Lamentation* of Guido Mazzoni, seven grieving figures around the body of Christ. (In their dynamism and psychological individuation, the terra-cottas call to mind Niccolò dell'Arca's *Lamentation* in Santa Maria della Vita, Bologna, a definite model for Mazzoni.) Alongside the Florentine art of Rossellino and Benedetto, this un-Florentine manner—more typical of Emilia-Romagna (Mazzoni was from Modena)—gains its place in the Monteoliveto pantheon.

Mazzoni's theater of grieving, amid which the viewer stands, includes a portrait of the artist's royal patron, Alfonso II, cast here in the role of Joseph of Arimathea. *"Ha un'aria terribile,"* Vasari says of the figure. *Terribile* as in *terribilità*: vastness, incommensurability, awe-inspiring greatness. A term—like "the sublime"—marking out a limit: beyond this not. When they still held their polychrome finish, these urgent grievers, so naturalistic in their attitudes, must have given a turn to all who saw them. Even the now earth-colored figures can momentarily fool the eye. As art historian George L. Hersey writes: "The poses and gestures are full of unself-conscious abandon. There is not the lightest idealization: each wrinkle and scar is sculptured with almost sadistic emphasis." He points out, also, that the figures are separate and movable and can be arranged in any composition around the body of Christ. By contrast to

Florentine models, there is here "no set of geometries within which the bodies are installed. The work is not only in an entirely differ-

ent style, it constitutes a different use of art," expressing the hardness and pitilessness of life, the frightfulness and *terribilità* of what life can do.

Hersey goes on to suggest that, when first seen in the 1490s, the figures of *The Lamentation* would have reminded at least some viewers of another, still more poignant

Detail of The Lamentation, *with Alfonso II as Joseph of Arimathea at left*

gallery of figures in Naples. Ferdinand I, Alfonso II's long-reigning father, had filled an exhibition hall of Castel Nuovo with the mummified remains of his enemies. Paolo Giovio, the sixteenth-century bishop, doctor, and biographer, writes in his *Historiarum sui temporis*: "They say that these dried cadavers were displayed, pickled with herbs, a frightful sight, in the dress they wore when alive and with the same ornaments, so that by this terrible example of tyranny, those who did not wish to be similarly served might be properly afraid."

FOUR

Particulars

For knowledge drawn freshly, and in our view, out of particulars,
knoweth the way best to particulars again.

—Francis Bacon, *The Advancement of Learning*

In June 2010, a team of researchers based in Ravenna assembled the international press to announce that they had identified, "with eighty-five percent certainty," the mortal remains of Michelangelo Merisi, known to the world as Caravaggio, taken from the crypt of a church at Porto Ercole in Tuscany. DNA samples from the bones had been successfully matched to those of persons named Merisi at Caravaggio, the Lombard village where the artist grew up in the last quarter of the sixteenth century. Displayed on red velvet to the press were part of a mandible, part of a rib, and part of a cranium. In the same season, an exhibition of twenty-five paintings by Caravaggio at Rome's Scuderie del Quirinale drew more than half a million visitors. Week after week, people waited for hours in the Roman sun for their turn to enter.

This artist, nowadays equal in interest to Rembrandt or Vermeer, Monet or Cézanne, went all but forgotten for three hundred years, his art a comet that astonished and then disappeared. Yes, there were the *caravaggisti* who followed him—Jusepe de Ribera, Bartolomeo Manfredi, Giovanni Battista Caracciolo, Artemisia Gentileschi, Hendrick ter Brugghen, the young Diego Velázquez— but by the 1630s Caravaggio's preeminence had died out in favor of Poussin, who was to the seventeenth century what Picasso was to the twentieth. Already in 1620, a decade after Caravaggio's early death, the Roman art patron Giulio Mancini writes about him and the *caravaggisti*: "One can see how much wrong the moderns do: if they decide to depict the Virgin, Our Lady, they portray her like some filthy whore from the slums." The argument that gained the day in the course of the seventeenth century was that Caravaggio had, unlike his great contemporary Annibale Carracci, lost faith in art and sought to substitute untransfigured nature for it (the inevitable case against any powerful new realism).

Still, Caravaggio's heightened chiaroscuro, somber glowing blueless palette, concentrated action, and meaty naturalism persisted thereafter in painting as a kind of underground song, anonymously nourishing artists who did not know they were his legatees. After the 1630s only the unusual Georges de La Tour consciously claimed the name of *caravaggista*. While Rembrandt never saw a painting by Caravaggio, he invented a particularized population we are accustomed to call "Caravaggesque" in its vivid corporeality and psychological persuasiveness, and in its lighting of earthen-colored figures against the darkness. But Poussin called Caravaggio the Enemy of Art. In the eighteenth century, he goes unmentioned in any of Joshua Reynolds's *Discourses*, a fair measure of the oblivion that had overtaken him. Who, looking at the greatest nineteenth-century realists before modernism—Goya, Delacroix, Courbet, Daumier—does not think of Caravaggio, though his was not a name any of these painters conjured with? He remained unheralded till 1905, when Roger Fry wrote: "There is hardly any one artist whose work is of such moment as [Caravaggio's] in the development of modern art. . . . He was indeed in many senses the first modern artist; the first . . . to proceed not by evolution but by revolution; the first to rely entirely on his own temperamental attitude and to defy tradition and authority. . . . His force and sincerity compel our admiration, and the sheer power of his originality makes him one of the most interesting figures in the history of art." What becomes clear over the course of the twentieth century is that Caravaggio turned away from the distancing conventions of his age in quest of the nerves and blood of moment-by-moment human experience. His Christ, his Virgin, his saints are unidealized flesh. They are us.

A journey to Naples' seventeenth-century Church of Pio Monte della Misericordia on via dei Tribunali is sufficient to make the case. There, behind the altar, is Caravaggio's *Seven Acts of Mercy*. The original commission, for seven canvases, he reconceived as one large picture encompassing all of the seven corporal acts the Church designates as redemptive: burying the dead, sheltering the homeless, feeding the hungry, giving water to the thirsty, attending the sick, visiting the imprisoned, and clothing the naked. Above the dynamic, tangled composition of the suffering and the compassion-ating, Caravaggio has tangled the divine-but-human Mother, Child, and angels who are the cause of all mercy. Most memorable to any-one who sees the painting are the two figures on the right. Exposing one breast, a daughter gives suck through a grate to her jailed father. Their faces, hers as she turns away, his as he sucks, have a terrible psychological accuracy: famishment and shame on the one, piety and revulsion on the other.

But there is a painting of still uncannier psychology, housed in Palazzo Zevallos Stigliano, home nowadays of a bank, Intesa Sanpaolo. (As you enter, note the opulent portal; it is by the great Baroque architect and sculptor Cosimo Fanzago, about whom more presently.) *The Martyrdom of Saint Ursula* is almost certainly Caravaggio's last work. Ursula, a fictitious third-century Germanic martyr, is said in *The Golden Legend*, Jacobus de Voragine's thirteenth-century compilation of hagiographies, to have been among eleven thousand virgins beheaded by the king of the Huns when they would not renounce Christianity. He offered clemency to Ursula on the condition that she marry him, and martyred her when she refused.

Caravaggio's canvas, completed in 1610 during his violent last stay in the city—his face had been slashed in another of the homicidal street brawls he tended to get into—was commissioned by the Genoese Marcantonio Doria, future prince of Angri. Five figures loom forth from the unmodulated darkness surrounding them. The king of the Huns wears puffed red sleeves, a high headdress, and a glittering cuirass reflecting a source of light on the left. Also lit is his right hand, which has just drawn and released the bow that sends the arrow point-blank into Ursula's chest. The lit side of his face reveals neither ruthlessness nor indignation—only withered age. Or is it a dawning horror at what he's done? Ursula looks down with either mild bemusement or a sad foreknowledge. Any number of visits to Palazzo Zevallos leave one no wiser. As art historian Michael Fried says: "It is all but impossible to put a name to the expression of any of the figures in the painting; by now Caravaggio has largely passed beyond the range of recognizable modes of human feeling." On the far right, the face of the armored and helmeted adjutant of the king is mostly turned away. But there is, at the center of the composition, a crone whose eyes, taking in the king, would seem to express immeasurable grief. To no avail, she has thrust her right hand (disclosed only recently when the picture was cleaned and the overpainting removed) between killer and victim. The feeling is of complete stillness, though the bowstring may still be vibrating. Time and eternity have intersected. Pierced by the arrow, Ursula seems sunk in sacred contemplation. It is a picture about final things, damnation and salvation transfixing the scene while at the rear a fifth figure, openmouthed and craning his neck for a better view, is unmistakably Michelangelo Merisi da Caravaggio himself.

Romanesque I love by instinct, Gothic by education. As for Renaissance, it is the perfection of European architecture. What could be more beautiful than Brunelleschi's Pazzi Chapel at Santa Croce in Florence, Bramante's Tempietto on the Janiculum in Rome, or, here in Naples, the Triumphal Arch of Alfonso the Magnanimous at Castel Nuovo? These are supremacies. And what of the international style that follows the Renaissance—the aggressively self-assertive Baroque of the Counter-Reformation, embodying Catholicism's declaration of all it has in the way of splendor and all that Protestantism lacks? It takes some getting used to, especially here, where its hypertheatrical Spanish version predominates. The eye is driven every which way. Unlike Romanesque with its contemplative otherworldliness, Baroque trumpets worldly reassurance. Unlike Gothic with its rational filigree, Baroque goes to extremes. Unlike Renaissance, with its humanist reverence, Baroque tears up the ancient canons of taste. Readers of Evelyn Waugh's

Brideshead Revisited will remember Charles Ryder's description of his conversion to the Baroque: "Here under that high and insolent dome, under those coffered ceilings; here, as I passed through those arches and broken pediments to the pillared shade beyond and sat, hour by hour before the fountain, probing its shadows, tracing its lingering echoes, rejoicing in all its clustered feats of daring and invention, I felt a whole new system of nerves alive within me, as though the water that spurted and bubbled among its stones, was indeed a life-giving spring."

Seated in the Church of San Gregorio Armeno, a fine example of the style, now finely restored, I have waited on such a conversion of my own, in vain. Charles Ryder I am not, and it may be that without the dawning of certain Catholic emotions, Baroque can be no more than dazzlements of the eye. The life-giving springs are elsewhere.

But if such a conversion *were* to overtake me, it would more likely be at the Charterhouse of San Martino, majestic on its hill overlooking the harbor. Much of what is most remarkable here is owed to Cosimo Fanzago, who came from Bergamo to the court of the Spanish viceroy at age twenty-two to work on the charter-

house and remained chiefly in Naples for the rest of his life. Within the cloister is the monks' burial ground, a rectangle of grass marked off by a marble balustrade adorned at regular intervals with what appear to be actual skulls—breathtaking marble carvings, in fact, of what remains when the flesh goes.

Monks' burial ground, cloister,
Charterhouse of San Martino

At one corner of the cloister, surmounting and overwhelming a pair of
doors at right angles to each other, are
two marvelously realistic busts of ecclesiastical figures, heroic in scale, larger
than the doors themselves. The statues
seem to have come to life in order to
lean out of their niches, and their blank
eyes follow you. It is this dramatic wedding of sculpture to architecture that is
Fanzago's great contribution. Within
the church of the charterhouse, all is
Baroque commotion—the polychrome
marble inlays adorning the floor and

*Busts of Saint Hugo and Blessed
Nicola Albergati, by Cosimo Fanzago,
Charterhouse of San Martino*

pillars, the creamy marble wavelets along the ornate communion
rail, the outsize silver angels frozen in flight at either end of the altar.
How different from the exterior. Take a moment, before going in, to
admire the dignified simplicity of the master's façade: square and
round windows, *piperno* pilasters against the white marble—right
angles and curves supremely harmonized.

Along the stretch of Spaccanapoli called via San Biagio
dei Librai is an unimposing shop where religious articles are sold:
dashboard Madonnas, a battery-operated Christ in agony, Day-Glo
versions of Leonardo's *Last Supper*, and other rubbish. Here, in the
latter decades of Spain's long rule, Giambattista Vico's father had
his bookshop, above which the family lived. One day in 1675, the
seven-year-old boy fell from a ladder, doubtless reaching for a book

on one of the higher shelves, and lay unconscious for hours. The local apothecary, examining the child, announced that if he survived he would be an idiot. Vico was frail all his life as a consequence of this fall, though certainly not weak of mind. *Principles of New Science Concerning the Common Nature of Nations*, on which his murky fame rests, is among the most original books in the history of European philosophy. As in antiquity Socrates brought thinking down from the heavens to the city, so Vico turns it from the immutable Cartesian principles of natural philosophy dominant in his day to the mutable truths of many societies at many different stages of development. This historicism—a point of view of which he is the father—finds the truth of human things in their becoming (*nascimento*).

Before Vico, philosophy had sought to pierce through changing appearances to an unchanging reality. But his revolutionary philosophical method seeks to grasp a changing reality—the stream of history, all that human beings have done and known and suffered—through the kaleidoscopically mutable means of human expression. Against his early master Descartes, Vico writes in 1708 that clarity and distinctness, the proper criteria for mathematics and natural philosophy (i.e., the physical sciences), are not the proper criteria for the world of man-made things—"the civil world," "polity," "this great city of the nations," this stream of history containing us and all we contrive. Vico's new science of human things (*le cose umane*) is an obvious affront to Cartesian rationalism, which regards historical knowledge as an oxymoron; the amalgam of travelers' tales, rumors, and fables is at best curious information. Descartes sees historians from Herodotus forward as purveyors of dubious wares. The greatest historian of Rome, he declares, knows no more than Cicero's servant girl knew. About the study of the classics, Descartes is derisive: "A man needs Greek or Latin no more than Low-Breton, to know the history of the Roman Empire no more than the smallest country there is."

Vico was nineteen when Newton published his universe-shattering *Principia* and twenty-seven when Leibniz published the *Système nouveau de la nature*; these and the preceding intellectual triumphs of seventeenth-century mathematics and science meant nothing to him. This math-challenged nobody made not knowledge that is mathematically demonstrable but knowledge that is genetic, historical, *per caussas* (his spelling), into a counter-argument, unheard beyond Naples. *"Verum et factum convertuntur"* sums it up: The true and the made are interchangeable, i.e., man can fully know only what he has made; perfect knowledge is of historical things. "The rule and criterion of the truth is to have made it."

This neatly turns Descartes on his head. For Cartesian a priori certainty is based on the *verum*, as Vico calls it, of clear and distinct ideas; Viconian knowledge, or *factum*, is an accumulated a posteriori certainty based on painstaking research into man-made things. Vico's outlandishly impudent anti-Cartesian argument is that it is only about these man-made things, not about nature, that we can have clear and distinct knowledge. Human beings like us made everything within the stream of history—the languages, religions, laws, cities; the poetry, art, and music—all the evidences of our having been here. These man-made things are modes or varieties (*modificazioni*) of the human mind (*mente*); being a human mind myself, I can know them, however remote they are from me in time and space. Vico's new science exalts humane knowledge, which is self-knowledge by way of the *modificazioni*, above the knowledge of nature. Because I possess the faculty of *fantasia*, or sympathetic imagination, I can by means of it enter into all things human. As Edmund Wilson glosses Vico: "The myths that have made us wonder are projections of a human imagination like our own and, if we look for the key inside ourselves and learn how to read them correctly, they will supply us with a record, inaccessible up to now, of the adventures of men like ourselves."

For Descartes, knowledge of the natural world was the paradigm of all knowing. Accordingly, knowledge of intentional, man-made things was less reliable, subscientific. The absolute daring of Vico's new science is to declare knowledge of human things superior to that of the natural sciences. What I can know most certainly, he writes, is what humans like me have made. Natural things I can know only from the outside; but intentional things I can know from within. (Echoing Vico, the nineteenth-century German philosopher Wilhelm Dilthey would distinguish between the *Naturwissenschaften* and the *Geisteswissenschaften*, the natural and the human sciences; from the one we get *Wissen*, knowledge, from the other *Verstehen*, understanding.) All of these things, unlike rocks, trees, clouds, oceans, stars, were made by human beings, and I am a human being too. Summing up the basic principle of Vico's *New Science*, Isaiah Berlin says: "We are men, and there is a spiritual affinity between us all, so that what one generation did or suffered, another can . . . comprehend as part of its own autobiography." All the *modificazioni* of what Vico variously called "humanity," "the civil world," "the great city of the human race"—everything having its origin and course and dissolution within the stream of history—is available to the hard work of *fantasia*, or imaginative knowing.

André Malraux, a man as glamorous and *mondain* as Vico was

weakly and obscure, made the argument in *Les voix du silence*, his anti–history of art, that nothing from the past is really recapturable and that we delude ourselves if we believe that what historical imagination reconstructs is anything more than a will to power over essentially unknowable monuments. Where the *New Science* is a call to grasp sympathetically what it has meant to be human in every time and place, *Les voix du silence* is a fancy, high-octane counsel of despair; when he rhapsodizes about works of art, Malraux is really rhapsodizing about himself. E. H. Gombrich, greatest of art historians, neatly handles him in a sentence: "There is an unfortunate resemblance between the Cretan, beloved of logicians, who asserts that everything a Cretan says is a lie, and the interpreter of art who says that everything we say about art is a myth." Nowadays the *New Science* and *The Voices of Silence* are equally unread. But for those of us in love with unread books, the choice between the two is not difficult. One gives off vibrant early-modern light; the other, late-modern smoke.

Vico's journey from Cartesian intellectualism to his own historicism—the reconciliation of philosophy to philology, universals to particulars—begins only in middle age. Impoverished, unrenowned, and lonely though his life was, it presents the spectacle of a decades-long self-metamorphosis and, best of all, a culmination in old age. (What writer does not wish his career to have this shape?)

Around a century after Vico's death, Jules Michelet, greatest of French historians, recovered the *New Science* from the utter oblivion it had fallen into, and became the first Viconian, basing his *History of France* on premises learned from the forgotten Neapolitan: "I had no teacher but Vico." What comes to dominate the nineteenth century, as powerfully as mechanistic models of physical nature had dominated the seventeenth, is historicism, the idea that the being of societies is their becoming and that to understand human things is to know them genetically, in all the particulars of their coming-to-be. So much a part of post-Enlightenment thinking—the common sense of two centuries now—is this historicism that it is easy to forget what an achievement it once was, carried out against the odds by a colossally original and poignantly lonely Neapolitan mind working in penurious obscurity and without honor in his lifetime.

This afternoon I'm taking a very long walk—all the way out to Posillipo, to the apartment of Shirley Hazzard, who has lived seasonally at Naples and Capri and knows the Bay fanatically well. I'm lucky enough to be having dinner with her. "Ring the bell and I'll come down the path to meet you." She's "the Meesus Shirley" to people in the streets, "Signora Steeg" (her late husband was the biographer and scholar Francis Steegmuller) to maître d's, and "La Hazzard" to the local press, particularly since being made an honorary citizen of Capri. Shirley is the most formidable talker I have ever known, more cataract than woman when she gets going, and everything she has to say is of interest. Aware of the exceptional demands she makes on the oxygen ("Just interrupt"), she's a heroic listener, too. Her talk is born not of self-importance but of an urgent need to clarify, and a still more urgent need to share the pleasure in what she knows. Mostly I have asked questions; without her answers I would understand much less of this bay.

The path is an alley of cypresses leading to a large establishment at the water's edge. In the guest cottage are rooms that Shirley and Francis rented for years and where she stayed on. She takes me immediately to the balcony, and I realize this is one of the places

I've regularly seen on the ferry ride to Ischia. Villa Rosebery, where Vittorio Emanuele III signed the instrument of his abdication in the spring of 1946, and now an official residence of the president of the Italian Republic, is next door. Right off Shirley's balcony, disappearing and appearing with the surge and retreat of the water, are ruins of one of the vast residences (vastest of all was Vedius Pollio's, he of the flesh-eating lampreys) that in Roman times covered this spit of land.

Shirley Hazzard, Capri, 1982

She gives me a prosecco and we sit down, after the customary modicum of small talk, to our preferred conversation—largely about the Neapolitan past. This evening I am full and overfull of Vico.

"The department of general ideas has never been a comfortable lookout for me," she says.

"I studied philosophy in college, even thought that might be my line of work. The more abstract an author, the better I liked him. Then one day something happened. I can remember exactly where I was, even the position I was seated in. I was reading a novel. No ordinary novel. It was *The Portrait of a Lady.* I'd come to the part where Isabel, betrayed and ensnared and used in Rome, goes back to the Touchetts' house in the English countryside. And cousin Ralph is upstairs on his deathbed. And he says to her, 'Remember this, that if you've been hated you've also been loved. Ah but, Isabel—*adored!*' And then they are beyond words. And I thought to myself: Two souls flooding each other to one level, mutual accord, the crown of life. So a novel can show that. Okay, philosophy is the love of wisdom, well and good. But here in literature was wisdom itself. Thus ended my affair with what you call the department of general ideas. For me it was stories, novels, and poems from then on. But the thing about Vico is that he among philosophers is the one who seems to know this, to know that particulars, not universals, are what matter." This evening, it appears that I am to be the talker.

"I tried to read him once," she says with a shake of her head.

"A haggis, I know. But with lumps of genius in it. The first enthusiasts for Vico were the Romantics, and it's been romantics ever since who've gone for him. But he's so unruly and vast that everything is in him, and everybody—Roman Catholics, liberal humanists, Marxists, existentialists, poststructuralists—can enter the labyrinth of his work and emerge with confirmation of the point of view they went in with."

On this early evening of late-summer sun, however, dinner is a more urgent topic than ideas. Shirley telephones to book a table at a nearby restaurant, order a taxi, and off we go.

Once we're seated and at our ease, I start in again on Vico, but she gives me a look that says it's her turn to talk now. The waiter brings menus. I propose a whiskey. "That is something I do only with men of my own generation," she says, setting me straight, "or the one before that," and orders a prosecco.

Some are tempted by the idea that Vico was only pretending to be pious, that a putative Catholicism gave cover to the godless Epicureanism at the heart of his teaching. He does seem to agree with Lucretius to the extent of positing men's beginnings not in Eden but as hideous giants (*grossi bestioni*) who only gradually civilized themselves. Having come to such heterodox conclusions, he had to hedge them in the *New Science* with his strange claim that the Hebrew forebears of the one true faith had not been such giants, had instead been descendants of Adam and Eve; only the so-called gentile nations—the non-Hebrews—had begun in barbarism. "First the forests, then the huts, thence the villages, next the cities, finally the academies," he says of the gentiles. The Hebrews, by contrast, begin in perfection.

As a young man he'd seen his less prudent friends, Epicurean worshippers of Lucretius and followers of French philosopher Pierre Gassendi, called before the Papal Inquisition for things they'd incautiously said. One Francesco Manuzzi, a Neapolitan witness for the Inquisition, denounced himself and his learned friends, detailing the blasphemies they'd entertained: "Before Adam there were men in the world, who were composed of atoms, as all the animals were; and the shrewder among them began to build houses, farms, forts and cities; and formed unions among themselves, some here, some there; and the shrewdest made themselves out to be sons of Saturn, Jupiter or some other god . . . in order to be honored and venerated by the people; and later, when Christ Our Lord came into the world, he was also ambitious to rule, and had himself declared the son of God, though he was not, and promulgated laws and got himself disciples and followers; and because the Hebrews knew he was an impostor, they had him taken and killed."

Whether the young Vico entertained such heresies himself is possible, not certain. What we do know is that his mature years— in which all of his major work was done—were passed in the company of priests and monks, men he relied on and needed. The heady

days of reading Gassendi and Lucretius and gathering with the like-
minded to talk of such things were far behind him, if indeed there
were such heady days. Still, those priests and monks would have been
scandalized to learn what an explosive mixture Vico was concoct-
ing in his *New Science*. For his Catholic piety and his historicism—
alternately urged in his masterwork—are mutually exclusive. He
manfully strives to have both by claiming, as I say, that the gentile
peoples developed out of *grossi bestioni*, while the Jews, because
they possessed the word of God (albeit without adequately grasping
it), were made in the image of God. Vico lived with a great insoluble
contradiction.

Whether he grasped it or not is one of the things *vichisti* go on
arguing about. The belief in Eden, original sin, God's love as proven
by Christ's death, resurrection, and promise that he will come again
to judge the living and the dead—this rectilinear sequence is incompatible with the belief that man turns himself, again and again over
the millennia, from a beast into a person. Vico's doctrine of cycles
of history—*corsi* and *ricorsi*—is inescapably heathen. Though he
insists that these cycles pertain only to the gentile nations, when his
prose grows most eloquent, he forgets to add this pious proviso,
and declares eternal recurrence of the development from savage
beginnings to decadent collapse (*sorgimenti, progressi, stati, deca-
denze, fini*), a recurring rather than rectilinear understanding of
human time, of history.

But what scholars in a specialized subdivision of the history of
ideas wrangle endlessly about, I cannot hope to settle. Specialized
scholars and absolutely no one else. At the center of the Villa Comu-
nale gardens stands a prominent landmark, the statue of Naples'
leading philosopher, Giambattista Vico, revered and unread.

. . .

On August afternoons, when the heat is African and the
sun seems to fill the whole sky, street-life dies away. Every shutter
is pulled to. Even the tradition of afternoon lovemaking, anciently
honored here in its licit and illicit forms, is in abeyance. Mario,
a lively fellow who lives upstairs and entertains a steady stream of
young ladies in the cooler months, tells me bluntly that in July and
August his ambitions go no further than "making the saw," collo-
quial Italian for masturbating.

For my part, I'm getting through the airless afternoons with a pile
of books about the Borboni—the last five kings of Naples, a lesser
branch of the same Bourbon stock who ruled France till the Revolution and again during the Restoration, and Spain till 1931, and
presided throughout the southern Italian peninsula and in Sicily
from 1734 to 1860 (with a nine-year Bonapartist interregnum). The
Kingdom of the Two Sicilies, as it was formally known after the fall
of the Napoleonic Empire and reestablishment of absolutist Bourbon rule here, was a byword for anticonstitutionalism, suppression
of dissent, antiquated religiosity, and all-around benightedness.

"They were goons," Shirley says, "but goons who built things."
Teatro San Carlo, the Museo Archeologico Nazionale, the Royal
Palace of Capodimonte, the Albergo dei Poveri (Royal Poorhouse),
the Church of San Paolo Maggiore, and other *grandissimi lavori* are
owed to them. Giuseppe and Donato Massa's triumphantly theatrical majolica cloister within Santa Chiara is perhaps the ultimate feat
of the whole period: the grand style touched up by whimsy. Charles
of Bourbon—son of King Philip V of Spain and his Italian second
wife, the enterprising Elisabetta Farnese—who claimed the throne

in 1734 and established the independent and autonomous Kingdom of the Two Sicilies, was responsible for these marvelous things,
still the highlights of any visit. Charles was additionally responsible
for making Naples the musical capital of Europe. It boasted in those
years the likes of Giovanni Battista Pergolesi, Domenico Cimarosa,
and Alessandro and Domenico Scarlatti, and hosted such emi-
nences as Pietro Metastasio, greatest of all librettists. "Run, fly to
Naples!" Rousseau recommended in the entry on "Genius" in his
Dictionary of Music, summing up the incomparable era of Charles
Bourbon. If one had to name a moment at which Naples was most
brilliant—the most exciting city in Europe—it would surely be this
reign, 1734–1759, after which, upon the death of his half brother
Ferdinand VI, Charles departed to become king of Spain and left his
third son, another Ferdinand—babyish, uneducated—to govern the
Two Sicilies. How brilliant Charles of Bourbon's Neapolitan time
had been, the reversals and degradations of the next hundred years
under Ferdinand and his successors would reveal.

My first view of Bourbon Naples was from a long way off. I was
about twelve, watching the late show in Fort Worth. The movie was
That Hamilton Woman, Alexander Korda's dressy propaganda
piece declaring against tyranny, whether Bonapartist or Hitlerian,
which appeared in the dark days before America's entry into the
Second World War. At twelve I understood none of that. What I
understood was simply what I saw: a smoking volcano, ladies and
gents in fantastic clothes, Laurence Olivier as the battered hero
growing more beautiful as first an arm goes, then an eye, and Vivian
Leigh (with still a lot of Scarlett O'Hara clinging to her) as Emma,
Lady Hamilton. The love story of Horatio Nelson and Emma Hamilton has the momentousness of living, breathing people propelled

into legend, who know that their private passions belong to history even as they writhe with them. This was borne in on me some years ago at the old British Library when I saw, in a display case holding some of England's most precious documents, the unfinished letter Nelson had begun to his beloved two days before the battle of Trafalgar, October 21, 1805, in which he fell, medaled and ribanded and an easy mark for French sharpshooters. Aware of the significance of the document, Emma had the presence of mind to record on the page that Hardy, the hero's lieutenant, had conveyed it to her. Then she added, in an access of grief: "Oh miserable wretched Emma. Oh happy and glorious Nelson."

Wretched she afterward was, imprisoned for debt and later driven into exile at Calais—stealing liquor, if the movie version is to be believed, she who had been the most renowned beauty of Europe and bosom friend of Maria Carolina, queen of Naples. *That Hamilton Woman* was my introduction to glamour and degradation. I didn't know that England's twentieth-century hero, Churchill, loved the movie on other grounds. He ordered it shown on the journey of HMS *Prince of Wales* to her rendezvous with the American flotilla bearing President Roosevelt to Placentia Bay, Newfoundland—what history records as the signing of the Atlantic Charter. We are told by H. V. Morton, who was on board, that in the wardroom of the blacked-out warship, on the eve of the historical meeting, Churchill wept without embarrassment during the last reel of the film (called *Emma Hamilton* in British release) when the dying Nelson says, "Thank God I have done my duty. . . . Kiss me, Hardy."

Churchill seems to have played some role in encouraging Korda to make the film, and that evening at sea was the fifth time he had seen it. (There are memorable earlier scenes in which

Nelson speaks, in Churchillian periodic sentences, of the "irresist-ible power," "untainted honour," "generous public sympathies," "unconquerable valour," and so on of the British people, and—scorning the Peace of Amiens, for which read "Munich"—thunders that one cannot make terms with dictators bent on world conquest.) When the lights went up, the prime minister, still wet-eyed, said to those assembled: "I thought this would interest you gentlemen, many of whom have been recently engaged with the enemy in mat-ters of equal historical importance. Good night!"

Happy and glorious Nelson is, atop his column in Trafalgar Square. But at Naples there are no such monuments. Here, his memory is execrated. In the triangular piazza dei Martiri, nerve cen-ter of Quartiere Chiaia, is a column dating from the unification of Italy that honors the republican martyrs of four rebellions: the vic-tory of Giuseppe Garibaldi and his Thousand in 1860, which ended 126 years of Bourbon rule, along with the three blood-drenched failures preceding it—the revolutions of 1848, 1820–1821, and 1799. This last gave birth to the short-lived Parthenopean Repub-lic, proclaimed by a coalition of liberal-minded nobility, profession-als, and intelligentsia after Ferdinand and Maria Carolina fled under Nelson's protection to Palermo as Napoleonic forces made their way to Naples. Within five months, French forces—"friends" of the Republic, who were killing it with their demands for reparations—withdrew and left to their fate the cohort of well-born, well-meaning liberals intoxicated by the noble rhetoric of the French revolution-ary example. Cardinal Fabrizio Ruffo's Sanfedisti, or Army of the Faithful, quickly mustered in Calabria and moved north in force to reclaim the capital for the Bourbons. Meanwhile, awaiting them within the city were the *lazzaroni*, ragamuffin foot soldiers of Crown and Church, a devotedly right-wing proletariat who laughed at new-fangled talk of *libertà* and longed only to restore the royal house. The king, who was uneducated, crude, and fun-loving, had always seemed to street Neapolitans one of their own; he was popularly celebrated as "Il Re Lazzarone," despite a way of life that of course had nothing in common with theirs. Ferdinand's tiny royal mind contained a single preoccupation, hunting in the Astroni crater and other royal game preserves. He was as silly as his father had been serious; affairs of state devolved almost entirely on the queen and her great ally, Prime Minister John Acton.

The elite who'd seized power in January of 1799 when Ferdinand and Maria Carolina fled were leading a revolution, under Jacobin colors, on behalf of a population who overwhelmingly did not want it. The *lazzaroni* loved the white banner with its Bourbon coat of arms, not the ugly *tricolore* of republicanism. After the Jacobins' last stand at Castel Sant'Elmo, after their agreement to Cardinal Ruffo's clement terms of surrender, after receiving his guarantee of safe conduct to Toulon, the defeated learned that prison or the scaffold was instead to be their fate. Maria Carolina—older sister to Marie Antoinette and sworn to avenge her—had through her friend and diplomatic conduit Emma, Lady Hamilton, asked Nelson, newly arrived in the Bay with his fleet, to punish the republicans, many of them persons of rank she knew, summarily and without mercy. Her words to Emma are memorable: "Finally, dear Milady, I recommend Lord Nelson to treat Naples as if it were an Irish town in a similar state of rebellion."

Which he did, ordering his men to remove rebels from the vessels bound for Toulon and incarcerate them in British ships. Especially memorable was the case of Commodore Francesco

Caracciolo, who had served the Bourbons with distinction, commanding the Neapolitan man-o'-war *Minerva*, before going over to the side of the short-lived Republic. Nelson's hastily convened court-martial allowed Caracciolo only to hear charges against him before he was hanged at midday from the yardarm of the *Minerva*. Nelson ordered him cut down at sunset. No retrieval of the executed man was permitted. In the surreal aftermath, Caracciolo's body, though weighted at the feet, resurfaced (from bloat, presumably) and seemed to all who saw him, including the newly returned king, to be making his way back to Naples. Terrified, Ferdinand ordered a Christian burial.

Ever glorious Nelson and forgotten Ruffo make a stark contrast. It was, after all, the latter who had actually restored the Bourbons. From her palace in Palermo, Maria Carolina's brutal recommendations made a mockery of Ruffo's terms of surrender. Meanwhile Nelson carried out her wishes in the judicial murder of Caracciolo, denounced afterward as such by Charles James Fox in the House of Commons. But for Nelson's services to the Bourbon cause, Ferdinand created him duke of Bronte and granted him the Bronte lands in Sicily. (Immensely impressed by this, a Yorkshire parson named Patrick Brunty began styling himself Brontë; thus two of England's greatest writers bear the name.)

A subsequent and more famous judicial murder comes to mind. All readers of Tolstoy's *War and Peace* remember the opening scene in which Pierre Bezukhov—an abstraction-loving boy-man with everything still ahead of him and everything still to learn—declares First Consul Bonaparte's recent execution of the

Duc d'Enghien, falsely accused of participating in a royalist plot to assassinate him, to have been "a political necessity." Pierre continues: "And it seems to me that Napoleon showed greatness of soul by not fearing to take on himself the whole responsibility of that deed." Such is revolution, such is history, says the unlovable fool whom every reader subsequently comes to love for the self-transformation that takes him from this immature shibboleth to true greatness of soul.

Enghien had been kidnapped from his residence at Baden and brought to the Château de Vincennes, east of Paris, which the First Consul was turning into a military encampment. There Enghien was subjected to a kangaroo court and summarily shot. It was the immediate prelude to Bonaparte's elevation of himself, on December 2, 1804, to emperor—his unironic rationale being that with such monarchist plots afoot, France's revolution could be protected only by a new line of royal blood—and it is from this moment that his Christian name, Napoleon, came into standard use. Although Great Britain's victory at Trafalgar had scotched French hopes of commanding the seas and invading the British Isles, Napoleon did achieve, six weeks later, an overwhelming land victory at Austerlitz against Russia and Austria—"The Battle of Three Emperors," as it is called—obliging Austria to withdraw from the Italian peninsula and permitting Napoleon to add "King of Italy" to his titles. In December of 1805, he denounced the existence of the Bourbon kingdom as "incompatible with the repose of Europe and the honor of my crown." Once again the Neapolitan royal family packed their thousands of trunks, looted the treasury, and fled to Palermo.

What had failed quickly in 1799 succeeded seven years later. This time the French had come to stay; they were better organized, better disciplined, and more understanding of the very un-French place they'd returned to. Napoleon named his brother Joseph king of Naples and, two years later, after sending him off to be king of Spain, replaced him with another relative, his brother-in-law Joachim Murat. It was an arrangement that would last until the restoration of Ferdinand and Maria Carolina by the Congress of Vienna in 1815.

Murat proved himself extraordinarily able, supplanting an anti-quated legal structure with the Napoleonic Code, curbing the pre-rogatives of the Church and the nobility, greatly expanding public education. Oil lamps like those of Paris, London, and Vienna now illuminated the streets. Naples' Botanical Garden, the largest in Europe at the time, was enriched; the Astronomical Observatory started at Capodimonte; and various conservatories united into the legendary Royal College of Music. The colossal budget deficit Ferdinand and Maria Carolina had left when they fled was eliminated. A modern postal system began operating. The right of divorce, hitherto unknown, was proclaimed. In the countryside, the ancient feudal system was definitively abolished.

Had Murat's brother-in-law not decided to invade Russia, these attractive developments might have produced a different trajectory for the South. But the era reached its spectacular end with Napoleon's retreat from Moscow, departure for and return from Elba, and final defeat at Waterloo in the late spring of 1815. He went to Saint Helena, Murat faced a firing squad, and Ferdinand—who would henceforth call himself King Ferdinand I of the Two Sicilies—returned with his morganatic wife, the duchess of Floridia (Maria Carolina having died in exile the previous year), to reclaim the kingdom. This dismal restoration outdid 1799 in repressiveness. Advocates of constitutionalism and freedom of the press were promptly driven into exile, imprisoned, or beheaded. A minimal constitution, belatedly granted in 1820, was annulled the following year. The right of divorce, so recently gained, was abolished. Books deemed Jacobin or heretical—the best, in other words, of the European Enlightenment—were burned, and a prohibitive tax imposed on all foreign literature. When Ferdinand died in 1825, after sixty-five years as king, he left to his ineffectual son Francis I the most antidemocratic and backward-looking monarchy in western Europe. The name Bourbon, associated in the great days of Charles Bourbon with enlightened values, had become in the course of Ferdinand's reign what it has remained: an international byword for reactionary brainlessness.

The death of Francis five years later brought fresh hopes with the crowning of his son Ferdinand II. In 1832, the appearance of a new quarterly, *The Progress of the Sciences, Letters and the Arts*, was tolerated. On the other hand, the general squalor and ignorance of even basic nineteenth-century hygiene facilitated a cholera epidemic in 1836–1837 that killed fourteen thousand people in the desperately crowded poorer quarters of Naples and more than a hundred thousand in the kingdom as a whole. Two years later, amid royal festivities and citywide celebration, Ferdinand II inaugurated the Naples–Portici railroad, Italy's first. But as its only purpose was to convey the royalty and their retainers back and forth, the line advanced no larger economic interests. This royal obliviousness to the technological potential of railroads tells much about life under the later Bourbons, and about why they were doomed. In 1845, Charles Dickens, like Englishmen before him, was captivated by the vitality and exoticism of the streets. "But, lovers and hunters of the picturesque," he wrote in his *Impressions of Naples*, "let us not keep too studiously out of view the miserable depravity, degradation, and wretchedness, with which this gay Neapolitan life is inseparably associated!"

The pan-European antimonarchist movements of 1848 had their genesis in Ferdinand II's kingdom. At Palermo, on January 12, revolutionary councils spontaneously sprang up in the aftermath of rioting. When the disorder spread to Messina, Ferdinand's response was to shell the city from the royal fortress, earning thereby the sobriquet by which he was thereafter known, "King Bomba." The rule of the councils in Sicily lasted sixteen months. Meanwhile revolution spread to most of the capitals of Europe in the short-lived realization of republican hopes known as the Springtime of Nations.

In a pamphlet published in 1851 and widely distributed in English, French, and Italian, William Gladstone, who had visited the kingdom, denounced Ferdinand II's monarchy as "an outrage upon religion, upon civilization, upon humanity, and upon decency . . . the negation of God erected into a system of Government." The pamphlet shocked Europe with its fabricated (this must be said) testimonies concerning the undoubted history of repressions and crimes committed by the crown. Increasingly, the monarchy lost control of events. "No state in Europe is in worse condition than ours," wrote Luigi Settembrini, one of the frequently imprisoned heroes of the antimonarchist movement. Then a new epidemic of cholera swept the kingdom in 1854–1855, killing nearly ten thousand in the capital alone. In 1856, when France and Great Britain appealed to Ferdinand to free the political prisoners who crowded his dungeons, the king's dismissive response provoked international sanctions. The French and British ambassadors were recalled, as were Ferdinand's envoys to Paris and London. In 1857, a massive earthquake leveled many of the towns of Basilicata, at the instep of the Italian boot. These calamities, poorly addressed by the monarchy, furthered northern European dismay and indignation.

In the spring of 1859, in the twenty-ninth year of his reign, Ferdinand II died. His successor, twenty-three-year-old Francesco—Franceschiello, "Little Francis," Francis II, as slender as his father had been fat—would last only fifteen months before the Savoyard army drove him and his "legitimist" forces north to the medieval fortress of Gaeta. History had passed Franceschiello and his lineage by. In Naples, Garibaldi and his Redshirts entered unopposed, unfurling banners bearing the emblem of the Piedmontese house of Savoy—henceforth the royal family of united Italy. From a window of via Toledo, he proclaimed the unification of the ancient fatherland. In the midst of these festivities, little attention was paid to the pathetic proclamation Francesco had issued to his subjects before fleeing: "As a descendant of a dynasty which has ruled this country for one hundred and twenty-six years, my affections are centered here. I am a Neapolitan, and cannot without feelings of bitter grief speak words of farewell to my dearly beloved people. Whatever may be my destiny, prosperous or contrary, I shall always preserve for them a lasting and affectionate remembrance. I recommend to them concord and peace, and the observance of their civic duties. Do not let an immoderate zeal for my fate be made a pretext for disorder."

After a siege at Gaeta lasting three months, Francesco's forces surrendered. A general amnesty was granted to the defeated survivors; most went home to Naples; some, after a period, joined the army of the united Italy they had lately fought. But the months in the fortress of Gaeta passed into legend. Francesco's nineteen-year-old wife, Maria Sofia, of the Bavarian royal house of Wittelsbach, had dressed wounds, comforted the dying, given away her own rations to the men. She'd organized a *carnevale* for the desperate troops. She'd mounted the battlements, musket in hand, to show herself to the enemy.

As part of the amnesty, when the end came, Francesco and his queen were granted an escort to Rome, still sovereign Vatican territory and not to be annexed for another ten years by the Savoyard crown. Under papal protection, they established a shadow court, vainly hoping for some new Congress of Vienna, or some new counterrevolution along the lines of 1849, to restore Bourbon rule to the South. Among the sad coterie surrounding them was Armand de Lawayss, a Belgian count who was the queen's lover—her first lover, since the marriage to Francesco had remained unconsummated because of his phimosis. When Maria Sofia found herself pregnant in 1862, she returned to her ancestral home at Possenhofen, where she gave birth in secret to a daughter immediately spirited away and

placed with Lawayss's family. Whether she ever saw the child again is unclear. The birth seven years later of a daughter by Francesco, who had undergone surgery for the condition that had kept the first decade of their marriage chaste, was the great joy of her life, though brief; the child died after only a few months.

United Italy's conquest of Rome in the same year, 1870, reduced the pope's once vast lands to a few acres, the little kingdom of Vatican City—and the spectral Bourbon court was driven into

Maria Sofia of Bavaria

a second exile, this time in Munich. Francesco died in 1894, after which Maria Sofia established herself at Neuilly-sur-Seine, Paris. Strange to say, her court there was frequented by anarchists and socialists. This Princess Casamassima–like radicalism—hard to explain given that her sister "Sissi," Empress Elisabeth of Austria-Hungary, had been stabbed to death in 1898 by an anarchist—has prompted wildly speculative claims about Maria Sofia, chief among them that she was the moving force behind the murder in 1900 of the Italian king Umberto I at Monza. That she had reason to hate the Savoyard monarchy and the united Italian state is clear. That she arranged for one Gaetano Bresci, an enraged anarchist residing in Paterson, New Jersey, to travel to Italy for the purpose of assassinating Umberto is something else again. The evidence, presented in 1999 in a book by Arrigo Petacco, is tantalizing but circumstantial.

Admittedly, Maria Sofia was mysterious. But such allegations as Petacco's are probably even further from the truth than Marcel Proust's beautiful idealization of her in *In Search of Lost Time*. The setting is the Paris house of M. and Mme. Verdurin, a pair of social-climbing salonistes who cover their ambitions with high aestheticism and who, along with the Baron de Charlus, are hosting a musical evening to showcase the talents of the gifted and amoral violinist Charles Morel, with whom Charlus is frantically in love. To revenge herself on the Baron for what she regards as a social betrayal, Mme. Verdurin tells Morel that association with such a man is ruining his reputation at the Conservatory; that people have taken to pointing him out as Charlus's catamite; that the old pouf is anyhow broke on account of blackmailers and can be of no financial use; that she understands that the Baron refers to him out of his hearing as "my servant." Every word is false, and all of it plausible.

Mme. Verdurin, one of the glittering gargoyles of world literature, knows by instinct how to drive the wedge between people she wishes to divide. As shabby as Charlus is splendid, she yet gains the day. "Leave me alone!" Morel shrieks at his lover and benefactor, then adds for the benefit of all present: "You know what I mean, all right. I'm not the first young man you've tried to corrupt!" Charlus reels back, heart-stabbed. The most gifted talker in Paris can mutter only a few desperate words.

It is at this point that the queen of Naples, having left her fan behind at the party and come to retrieve it, enters the Verdurins' drawing room again and quickly grasps the nature of the cruelties in progress. Brushing aside the sycophantic attentions of Mme. Verdurin, she makes straight for the Baron: "You do not look at all well, my dear cousin," she says. Whereupon the queen glares witheringly at Mme. Verdurin and Morel beside her. "Lean on my arm," she tells Charlus. "Be sure that it will support you. It is strong enough for that. You know that in the past, at Gaeta, it held the mob at bay. It shall be your rampart."

In 1984, the remains of Maria Sofia and Francesco, along with those of their infant daughter Cristina, were brought to Naples for re-interment in the Bourbon chapel of Santa Chiara.

Back at the glorious beginning, five kings earlier, Charles Bourbon's first great achievement had been the Teatro San Carlo, hailed as the most splendid opera house in Europe when it opened on the feast day of San Carlo Borromeo in 1737 with the premiere of Domenico Sarro's *Achille in Sciro* (libretto by Metastasio). The house quickly became an essential destination for musicians and music lovers. In 1770, the fourteen-year-old Mozart was here. Among the great premieres were Rossini's *Elisabetta, regina d'Inghilterra* (1815) and—following speedy reconstruction after a fire gutted the house—*Armida* (1817), *Mosè in Egitto* (1818), and *La donna del lago* (1819), all with the leading phenomenon of the day, Isabella Colbran. Later, under Ferdinand II, Donizetti's *Lucia di Lammermoor* (1835) and *Roberto Devereux* (1837) and Verdi's *Luisa Miller* (1849) were also first performed here.

After twenty or thirty evenings at the San Carlo, I've grown fascinated by an unaccompanied woman of a certain age who unfailingly attends. She seems to have made herself fundamental to the place. *Alta borghesia*, as they say, a person of elegance and obvious refinement; yet she is for some reason, I observe, a pariah among her class. In the atrium, she greets people who are plainly not pleased to see her. The dresses she turns up in are the haute couture of fifty and sixty years ago: Chanel, Balenciaga, Schiaparelli. Though large, she wears these with considerable panache. There is a positive sexiness to her, a whiff of the autumnal Ava Gardner, and Ava is what I've taken to calling her. She knows how to move on her high heels, then how to halt and pose. She is a bigger-boned, more ragged Ava. What attention men must have paid when first she wore these sublime creations. But the crowd at the San Carlo have been looking at them for too long now, and I seem to be her only fan here.

We hurry to our seats. A harp recital is on the boards this evening. The lively bright-eyed Frenchman who comes on to polite applause may not know he has entered the lions' den. He and his harp look terribly exposed up there. A few experimental pluckings to verify that the instrument is in tune, and he launches into a transcription of J. S. Bach's Suite for Lute. A murmur of approval ripples through the house. But some minutes later, from a box of the fourth ring, comes dissent in the form of a hacking cough. Our harpist finishes undeterred and sketches a quick bow.

Now for something less tried-and-true—Albert Roussel. Coughs. Throat clearings throughout. And are those mittens they're applauding in as the harpist takes a second bow? The Roussel has not been a *succès fou.*

But then our soloist's stock rises on the opening chords of a Debussy prelude, followed by two piano works, also by Debussy, transcribed for harp, the latter of which produces even a cry of *"Bis!"* from the throng. We file out for refreshment.

In the lobby, I watch Ava make her usual one-sided conversation with people eager to get loose of her; then I step out onto the sidewalk for a breath of air. A Gypsy child rushes at me with *"Bello signore!"* and thrusts out her hand. *"Monete!"* I give her my pocket change and hurry in to take my seat. Now our nervous-looking soloist comes back onstage. Fingers crooked below his chin, he asks our indulgence for the modernist music of André Caplet, Luciano Berio, and Benjamin Britten. Roaring silence from the crowd. Grim-faced, he seats himself at the harp and attacks Caplet's "Divertissement à l'espagnole." This is difficult music, all right. From the audience comes an accompaniment of women's handbags opening and closing. Someone's walking stick falls to the floor, then someone's umbrella. At the bow, our soloist winces at a catcall.

He courageously resumes his seat for something more modernist still, Berio's "Sequenza II." This music turns loose the Neapolitan id. There are boos, impersonations of flatulence. At the conclusion our hero bows elaborately, facetiously, then sits back down to Britten's Suite in C Major, which is glorious, whether Naples knows it or not. At the sparkling finish, I stand up to bang my hands together, but someone else is on her feet ahead of me. It's Ava—a friend to modernism, it turns out, hollering *"Bis! Bis!"* in a massive baritone. Am I the last person here to have figured out that she's male? I want to take her to supper. I want her to show me *her* Naples—a cross-dressing demimonde I've never glimpsed. I want to high-hat these philistines with Ava on my arm.

FIVE

Siren Calls, Siren Echoes

Our gods reflect the hearts that make them.

—Norman Douglas, *Old Calabria*

A *nineteenth-century resident of Capri,* Colonel John
Clay MacKowen, likened the island to an old boot. Turn the
map east side down and you'll see what he meant: "The shape of
an old cavalier's boot, and Nature in a lavish mood has given
it even a spur." Like many who've called Capri home, J. C. Mac-
Kowen sounds more made-up than real. Scion of a slave-owning
New Orleans family, a veteran who had fought by the side of
Robert E. Lee, he was so disgusted with the outcome of the War
Between the States, specifically with the loss of his family's chattel
wealth, that he left America for Europe. A decade later, having quali-
fied as a physician in Germany, he ventured to Capri on holiday and
fell irretrievably in love with the place. It is a familiar story among
the foreign colony, from antiquity to the present. Octavianus, not yet
Caesar Augustus, first of many a sacred monster to attach himself
to the island, in 29 B.C. traded Ischia, a possession nearly five times
larger, for Capri. Upon his first arrival, Suetonius reports, a withered
holm oak had miraculously put forth new growth, convincing the

emperor that here was the great good place. He returned frequently throughout his reign. His collection of skeletal remains purporting to be prehistoric beasts, along with gigantic weaponry and bones believed to belong to the mythic Teleboae, was established here— the prototype of every subsequent museum of natural history. In the summer of the year 14, nearer to death than he knew, Augustus sought repose and amusement among the natives, ordering Greeks to wear the toga and speak Latin and Romans to put on the chiton and speak Greek. On the way back to Rome a few days later, he fell ill and died at Nola, north of Naples. An epoch was marked, his stepson Tiberius assumed power, and Capri entered upon the most famous phase of its history.

Of Tiberius, everybody knows the alleged infamies. If we are to believe his great detractors—Tacitus and, especially, Suetonius— no sexual cruelty was beyond him. By their account, he favored the island chiefly as a hideaway in which to indulge his myriad perversions—unweaned infants forced to suck the imperial mem- ber, boys and girls raped, tortured, and thrown to their deaths from the heights of Villa Jovis, largest of his twelve palaces on the island, and so on. (Gilles de Rais, who in the fifteenth century murdered perhaps as many as eight hundred French children, said his inspira- tion had been Suetonius's life of Tiberius.)

The whole truth about Rome's second emperor, Norman Doug- las used to say, is in papyri locked beneath the lava of Herculaneum, awaiting further excavations (for which no one should hold his breath). Meanwhile, scholars of our own times have not taken seri- ously the fiendish depictions of Tacitus and Suetonius, who wrote their chronicles a few generations after Tiberius, and were fiercely anti-Julio-Claudian. It is as if the unquestionable ghastliness of some of his successors—Gaius Caligula, Nero, Domitian—had bled back onto Tiberius's own reputation, as onto that of his mother, Livia. But with all due respect to Robert Graves, the great exception among modern skeptics, evidence for his depravity appears no stronger than the traditional claims for Livia's archcriminality. The real Tiberius was an exemplary soldier and a very able if dour and anticharismatic ruler who seems to have come to Capri in his sixties not for debauchery but to escape the eternal Roman infighting. No vacation spot as it had been for Augustus, the island was instead his home year in and year out; for more than a decade the empire was administered from here. Semaphore and heliograph by day, fire signals by night, and a continuous traffic of envoys up and down the coast sustained the flow of information. It was from here that Tiberius ordered the death of Sejanus, having learned of the Praetorian prefect's ambitions against him.

Colonel MacKowen, perhaps a bit of a Roman emperor at heart, certainly every inch an old Louisiana Bourbon, established himself, as had Augustus and Tiberius before him, in residences around the island. He carried a bullwhip, employing it as liberally on *capresi* as if they were his slaves back home. Afterward, he'd munificently send round food to those he had lashed. *"Ciacca et mmereca,"* the islanders called him—"He strikes and he heals."

To be fair, MacKowen did also gain their affection as a dispenser of treatment and medicines at no charge. And one is even less willing to hate the man after reading his monograph on Capri, the first work of its kind. Printed at Naples in 1884 by compositors who knew not a word of the English they were setting and who blundered on nearly every page, it is a book collector's rarity, on paper so acidic you destroy the pages as you turn them. The original owner of my copy, whose name I can't make out, added "May, 1887, Capri" beneath his or her signature. I keep it in a box, as the binding has given way and the pages are chipped and broken.

The old anti-emancipationist loved every ruin and cove. His unmistakable Pompeii-red house up at Anacapri—a Moorish delight elaborated around a sixteenth-century Aragonese watchtower from back when Capri kept the lookout for corsairs—is today a higgledy-piggledy, unvisited museum housing the Neolithic ax helves and jadeite knives and other things the Colonel unearthed.

A word he caused to be incised into the façade, APRAGOPOLI, "City of Do-Littles," had evidently been Caesar Augustus's nickname for the island. Having little to do myself, I venture up there. Casa Rossa, as it is called, is ideal in the sleepy afternoon for illicit assignations, and this is exactly what I believe I've flounced into. The man passes me black looks and his much younger lady averts her face. A repeat of my embarrassment at Virgil's tomb, though here at least no skirts are up or trousers down.

Nothing natural or human failed to win MacKowen's curiosity. He was, like Norman Douglas a generation later, one of those inspired amateurs who honored the island with their intellectual insatiability, turning over every rock, venturing up every crag, entering every cave; who, seeing all there is to see, fret that they cannot enter the Grotta Oscura, too, sealed up in the early 1800s in a landslide.

"There was no butcher," MacKowen reports, "and beef could be obtained only when a cow had the misfortune to fall over a precipice," whereupon a trumpet call announced meat for sale in the Piazzetta. He is witty on the twenty-five-hundred-year-old rivalry between the lower town (Capri) and the upper town (Anacapri), a case of Freud's "narcissism of small differences" if ever there was one: "The people of Anacapri consider the air of Capri woefully deleterious to all moral principle, and wonder how an honest stranger can remain any length of time among such corrupted and evil specimens of humanity." (There is a local term of abuse unmentioned by MacKowen: *ciammiello*, referring to a boy from the upper town who's been duped into marrying a girl from the lower town.) And the Colonel is suddenly moving when he salutes the forbearance and strength of the island's women, alone much of the year while their husbands fished far out at sea for coral. Most of the heavy labor on land was accomplished by women negotiating the Scala Fenicia that zigzags up the face of Monte Solaro. "All the houses of Capri," says MacKowen, "have been carried to their present sites on the heads of women." He must have made that journey himself a thousand times, and grasped the arduousness of what was but a day's work for those indomitable Capriote wives. I myself recommend descent of the Phoenician Stairway to only the vigorous, and the upward climb to no one, having seen my life pass before my eyes the one time I tried it.

All told, the Colonel seems a decent man despite himself, generous with his medical expertise, loyal to the local women he lived with and the natural children they presented him with. But his end, it is said, was ignominious. Back in New Orleans in the summer of 1901, this MacKowen fell to bloviating nostalgically in a bar about slavery times, whereupon a former slave shot him to death. There are several reasons to doubt the account. All we can say with certainty is that John Clay MacKowen is buried in the city of his birth, and descendants of his live on Capri to this day.

. . .

The Scala Fenicia (not Phoenician at all, in fact demonstrably Greco-Roman) has been rebuilt repeatedly over the centuries. Prior to the construction of the Anacapri highway, it was—apart from a death-defying path called the Passetiello—the upper town's only link to the lower. This ancient stairway has its modern counterpart in via Krupp, a narrow pedestrian route from the Gardens of Augustus down to the Marina Piccola. After being closed for decades, the renovated via Krupp reopened in June 2008. Roberto Pane, architectural historian, preservationist, and toughest critic of ill-considered building and ill-judged restoration on the Bay, called the Krupp road a work of art, and if "work of art" means a thing inexhaustible to contemplation, then work of art it is. Instead of zigzagging rigidly down the Castiglione cliffside, it obliges irregularities in the living rock; you sense the rises and dips along the narrow route as you descend. The angle of vision is new at each hairpin turn.

Via Krupp's low tufa parapet is of rounded blocks, and a mortal temptation to young daredevils who try to walk it tightrope-wise. Beauty and danger have in fact kept close company on this face of the Castiglione hill for more than a century, ever since the brief, tragic phosphorescence of Fritz Krupp, who built the wondrous road. As sole—if reluctant—heir to his father's munitions industry, Friedrich Alfred Krupp commanded the largest private fortune in Germany, greater even than that of Kaiser Wilhelm II. Scholarly, fat, short-sighted, and asthmatic, Fritz had been the family embarrassment. This disapproval did not impede him from extraordinary success at the armaments trade once he'd turned himself to it. He earned a seat on the Kaiser's Privy Council. A marine biologist by avocation, Fritz came to the Bay in 1898 at the invitation of Dr. Anton Dohrn— founding head of the Naples Aquarium, at that time the world's finest collection of specimens. Having outfitted a pair of yachts with the latest marine research equipment, Krupp showed up minus his wife and two daughters, and checked into the Quisisana, the "Here One Gets Healthy," leading hotel of Capri from that day to this, an entire floor of which was let to him and his retinue. The name of the lodgings alone must have made a strong appeal; his asthma was worsening, and doctors back at Essen had recommended a Mediterranean sojourn.

"In his romantic eyes," Norman Douglas observed, "the inhabitants of Capri were children of nature, one and all of them." The truth was and is a lot more equivocal than Krupp's romantic eyes saw. When a generous man of unlimited means arrives in such an insular place, handing out gold coins at the quayside, nothing is afterward the same; thus it was at Capri. Fritz's preference for the Quisisana over the competing hostelry fed existing feuds. In general, those whose lives were enriched by the magnate worshipped him as a new Caesar. Those he'd not patronized increasingly wished him harm. Without knowing it, Krupp balkanized Capri into pro- and anti-Krupp camps.

In 1901, in a gesture of gratitude for Capriote hospitality, he purchased a parcel of land adjacent to the Carthusian monastery and terraced and planted it as a *giardino pubblico*—today's Gardens of Augustus. Below, the Krupp road to the Little Marina was simultaneously constructed. Secreted halfway down was the Grotto of Brother Felice, originally home to an early-fifteenth-century hermit, industrious and mathematically gifted, who over the course of thirty years had delved a pair of chambers from the rock face. Afterward monastic dormitories, and later a prison, the Grotta di Fra Felice had been abandoned—and, it would seem, forgotten—till Krupp adorned the exterior with ambulatories and terraces and pergolas and, within, fashioned a dining room, a kitchen, and lavatories, all of it with a view to evenings reviving the ancient imperial splendors and recreations.

These latter seem to have been Fritz's undoing. Among the southern charms he'd hearkened to was the available beauty of Capri's boys and young men. He had come from a country where homosexuality was, as in Great Britain, against the law and punished by prison at hard labor; his belated realization of his own nature, and of his freedom in Italy to act on it, proved overwhelming. At Krupp's splendidly refurbished Grotta di Fra Felice, according to one historian of these murky goings-on, handsome young *capresi* "submitted to sophisticated caresses from him, while three violinists played. An orgasm was celebrated by sky-rockets." Ludicrous, yes, and more than a little reckless, inasmuch as Fritz had the festivities photographed. Images found their way to a local pornographer, whose clientele were quick to observe that some of Krupp's acolytes fell short of the age of consent.

By stages, the press—first in Naples, then in Rome, finally in Germany—grew bolder in exposés of these goings-on. *La propaganda*, a leftist Neapolitan daily, ran a series detailing how this exploiter of the proletariat enjoyed himself. In Rome, *Avanti!* took up the hue and cry, as did *Vorwärts* in Berlin.

Back at Essen, Krupp sued the latter paper for libel. But when it became clear that the Kaiser would not come to his defense, he seems to have lost heart. Official reports attributed his death to an aortal aneurysm; but few have ever doubted that on the afternoon of November 22, 1902, Seine Exzellenz Herr Friedrich Alfred Krupp took his own life.

After an espresso this morning in the Piazzetta, where all of Capri forgathers—Europe's best drawing room, people call it—I head up via Roma, then down via provinciale Marina Grande, greeted by *"Salve,"* stopping to talk to an occasional cat or dog, wondering at the robust elderly folk who daily toil up and down these paths. I'm on what is, for me, an inevitable mission. The Cimitero Acattolico draws me. Cemeteries everywhere do. As a young man visiting Paris, I squandered money budgeted for food in order to take flowers to Stendhal and Heinrich Heine in Montmartre Cemetery; Proust and Wilde and Colette at Père Lachaise; Baudelaire at Montparnasse. At Highgate, in London, I made speed, roses in hand, for George Eliot's resting place (little visited by comparison with the bombastic tomb of Marx nearby). At the Old Jewish Cemetery of Prague, I dispensed with flowers, as this is not the Jewish way, instead laying a pebble on the grave of Rabbi Loew, who concocted the Golem and made it speak. At Asolo, I gave red tulips to Duse.

What harm does such silliness do? Piety is not the worst emotion for a youngster to get carried away with. And if I've outgrown the floral tributes, I will never outgrow the pleasure of tombs. When I found out that the Etruscans typically sited their necropolises, like the vast one at Cerveteri, so that the city of the living could continually contemplate the city of the dead, I decided with D. H. Lawrence that those pre–Greco-Roman inhabitants of Italy must have been the wisest human beings who ever lived.

In Capri's Cimitero Acattolico you may do homage to the gamut
of Anglo-American and other expatriates who took their pleasures
here, quarreled operatically, loved, envied, hated, desired, used, and
betrayed one another. Death has folded them in a common party, as
the poet says. In this non-Catholic ground, alongside the moder-
ately to greatly gifted, rest assorted hangers-on of Capri life: spong-
ers, climbers, holy fools, artistic phonies, Nazi propagandists—and
not least, enabling the show, provisioning it, the very rich, who are
always with us.

Take the Misses Wolcott-Perry, over by the north wall, side by
side in their choice location. Nothing but the best for Saidée Wol-
cott and Kate Perry, cousins propelled by real estate back in Iowa. To
solemnize the bond, they conjoined their surnames. (In *Vestal Fire*,
Compton Mackenzie's deliciously nasty satire of the social and sexual antics of Capri, they turn up as Virginia and Maimie Pepworth-
Norton.) The Lucullan hospitality of these two was counted among
the wonders of the Bay. From Villa Torricella, social omphalos of
the island in the early years of the last century—and with its Moorish minaret and tower still the most salient structure above Marina
Grande—they ruled the roost, ushering into or banishing from the
little universe of island society whomever they chose. Run afoul of
the Misses Wolcott-Perry and woe betide you.

There along the wall, in a rather sunken grave, lies Jacques
d'Adelswärd-Fersen, the pretty, foppish lightweight championed
by Kate and Saidée Wolcott-Perry as if he were a Valéry or a Rilke.
Having done time in France for inciting a minor to debauchery,
Fersen arrived in Capri in 1904, elevated himself from baron to
count, checked into the Quisisana, and consecrated his large hereditary income to construction of a villa perched at the northeastern

precipice of the island. "Sanctuary of Love and Sorrow," as the façade announces in Latin, Villa Lysis was the scene of Fersen's regrettable attempts at literary creation, and of his idolization of an out-for-the-main-chance Roman construction worker named Nino Cesarini. The pathetic finale came in 1923, when Fersen mixed himself a lethal cocktail of wine and cocaine, the latter of which he'd been addicted to for years. I do not recommend taking anyone you love up the winding path to Villa Lysis, the only thing of lasting interest that Fersen produced. It is a monument to folly and humiliation, and "Sanctuary of Delusion" would be a truer motto to have set above the door.

Over there, among these big spenders, lies poor John Ellingham Brooks. "Came for lunch and stayed for life," as he liked to tell people. Having arrived in 1895, he remained till his lonely death in 1929. Handsome, Cambridge-educated, bursting with the gospel of an empty aestheticism, he'd been the first lover of W. Somerset Maugham, in so many respects his polar opposite. Neither industrious nor skillful nor shrewd, Brooks was one of those would-be writers who indefinitely postpone; he didn't so much want to write as to already have written. How awed he must have been by his younger friends Maugham and E. F. Benson, so prolific and successful. The proximity to their industry and renown seems to have sufficed; it often does for would-be writers—a dreary and familiar pattern. As for what Maugham made of Brooks, we have the following: "He can discover nothing for himself. He intends to write, but for that he has neither energy, imagination, nor will. . . . He has a craving for admiration. He is weak, vain, and profoundly selfish." Brooks's brief marriage to the painter Romaine Goddard, thereafter famous as Romaine Brooks, resulted in an annuity of three hundred pounds, on condition that she never have to set eyes on him again, money that enabled him to go in with Maugham and Benson on the lease of Villa Cercola, at the eastern edge of Capri town. The two writers came and went; Brooks stayed, feeding the pets, making stabs at translation, playing the piano execrably. In lieu of CAVE CANEM, the warning carved elegantly into the threshold of Villa Cercola reads CAVE HOMINEM. And there was reason for the rest of the Anglo-American colony to beware the man. He'd been a tape recorder all those years, and over the course of many long evenings told Compton Mackenzie the stories that would constitute *Vestal Fire.* Thus his creativity was satisfied.

It is touching that a man who published nothing should have tagged along with the likes of Maugham, Benson, and Mackenzie—men who brought out books by the bushel. Maugham captured Brooks's exceptionally pathetic last years on the island in a heartless short story called "The Lotus Eater," in which a perfectly ordinary man dedicated to nothing but his pleasure declines from bohemianism to rancid poverty. The lotus eater ends his days as a mad scarecrow who darts from olive tree to olive tree. Brooks didn't actually go mad, but he did grow more and more spectral, dying alone of untreated cancer in a one-room shack on the island. This seems to have pleased Maugham very much. How anybody, so many years later, could harbor such hatred for a first love is hard to grasp.

Two rows away from Brooks lies Viet Harlan, director of the preeminent Nazi propaganda film, *Jud Süss.* But enough about the disagreeable, the pathetic, and the wicked. Over here is the distinguished-looking grave of Gracie Fields—Dame Gracie, as she became not long before her death. In war and out, she'd consoled and delighted millions with her no-nonsense Lancashire manner and wonderful renditions of "Sally," "Wish Me Luck As You Wave Me Good-bye," "The Biggest Aspidistra in the World," "Angels Guard Thee," "Christopher Robin Is Saying His Prayers," not to mention "The Isle of Capree." She lived here for decades, greatly loved.

But what I've come for this morning is to visit that tomb down there, the one inscribed *"Omnes eodem cogimur,"* a tag from Horace meaning, in loose translation, "Where all must gather." The least delusory, least sentimental epitaph on record, it was chosen by the great man who sleeps beneath it, a denizen of antiquity nobly, sometimes hilariously, displaced into the nineteenth and twentieth centuries: Norman Douglas, quoted several times already. Simultaneously Epicurean and Stoic, he summed up the Hellenistic excellences. Aristocratic by birth and rearing, he could as readily live rough as in style, and hadn't the ghost of a care for respectability or convention. If there was an amorality to him—that he couldn't stay away from prepubescent boys—there was also a grand gift for friendship with those who'd been in his bed, as well as those who hadn't. Graham Greene revered Douglas and sought, during seasonal sojourns at Capri, to adopt his attitude to life: "Find everything useful and nothing indispensable. . . . Find everything wonderful and nothing miraculous." They were an unlikely pair: Douglas, atheist, homosexual, poor, and madly interested in everything Parthenopean; Greene, Catholic, consecrated to women, rich, and indifferent to the Bay, where he came only to write his books.

Norman Douglas fathered forth the sensibility of English travel writing. Figures such as Robert Byron, Peter Fleming, Norman

Lewis, Patrick Leigh Fermor, Jan Morris, Bruce Chatwin, Colin Thubron, and Pico Iyer are his progeny. Bright-heartedness, fanatical curiosity, and flying wit are their shared talismans—along with willingness to be "a slave of [the] journey's emotions," as Robert Byron puts it. These powers they inherit from the author of *Old Calabria*, *Siren Land*, and *Alone*.

Edward Hutton, another of Douglas's inheritors, if a now forgotten one, said that "Uncle Norman" much preferred fact to emotion. I would say, rather, that it was the accurate emotions for flora, fauna, places, and people—the genii of nature and history deciphered—that drew him. On his first visit, he climbed one of the Faraglioni—steep crags standing offshore—in search of the blue lizard that lives only there, and netted a specimen. He scoured every square foot of Monte San Costanzo, looking, in vain, for a trace of the Doric temple to Athena known to have stood there in remote antiquity. He loved this bay as learnedly and athletically as anyone before or since, feeling that here if anywhere was the just proportion between what nature has made and humankind has added.

Norman Douglas and Graham Greene, Capri, circa 1948

And it loved him back in full measure. In her memoir *The Heart to Artemis*, Bryher (Annie Winifred Ellerman) describes his disembarkation at Capri's Marina Grande after an absence of eight years: "The news of his arrival spread from mouth to mouth. I have never seen a political leader enjoy so great a triumph. Men offered him wine, women with babies in their arms rushed up so that he might touch them, the children brought him flowers. I slipped away as he walked slowly through a crowd of several hundred people, shouting jokes in ribald Italian, kissing equally the small boys and girls and patting the babies as if they were kittens. The *signore* had deigned to return to his kingdom and I am sure that they believed that the crops would be abundant and the cisterns full of water as the result." I try to imagine any American or British writer today, of whatever eminence, being treated anywhere as well, but cannot. Douglas deserved it and more for having understood something profound about the Italian South and having embodied it in his vivid books: eternal paganism subsisting beneath the Christianity.

The mystery cult of Mithras, perhaps of Zoroastrian origin, into which men, and only men, were inducted, was brought to Rome from the East by returning soldiery. Its archaeological evidences have been found beneath a number of Rome's paleo-Christian churches (San Clemente, Santa Prisca, others), and it particularly appealed to Douglas for its obvious isomorphisms with Christianity, the competing Oriental dispensation that finally stamped it out. Mithraism included baptism, sacramental bread and wine, renunciation of the old life for the new, martyrology, final judgment. A canny copycat, primitive Christianity appropriated these things from its male-only competitor, much as it took from the worship of Cybele, great mother goddess of Asia Minor, embodiment of fertility, and venerated primarily by women, the washing away of sin and promise of new life—with not water but blood, in the Cybelean rite, pouring down onto the head of the neophyte when a sacrificial bull was slaughtered. Mithras is a name for the nourishment of the Sun, and Cybele for the endlessly fertile renewals of Earth the Mother. "Mithra, like Christ, is the 'Light of the World,'" says Douglas, "and Cybele, his whilom associate, is the Madonna or *Gran Madre di Dio*, the Magna

Mater of old, who was worshipped both at Capri and Sorrento."
So whatever it thought it was doing, Christianity in fact put new
wine into old bottles. The Light of the World had been Mithras, as
the Mother of God was Cybele.

Two images, of course, are everywhere you look hereabouts—
the one a young god hanging on a cross, the other a mother goddess
with a babe in arms. Among his great contributions, Douglas understood the backward abysm in this iconography, grasped the exquisite persistence of pagan, earthbound emotions among his beloved
southerners.

Our notion of the ancients is put together out of careful scholarship and inspired surmises. So much of who they were has perished. We see Greco-Roman antiquity through a glass darkly.
"A black gulf yawns," Douglas says, "between them and ourselves;
however clearly they wrought or thought, their personalities glide
away from us with the swiftness of a dream." Still, Douglas puts me
in mind of the mage-like professor of Giuseppe Tomasi di Lampedusa's great tale "Lighea" (translated as "The Professor and the
Siren"), who, in defiance of time's effacements and mutilations, has
uncannily possessed the whole of antiquity. How? It emerges that
in youth he took a Siren as his lover: "Suffice it to say that in those
embraces I enjoyed both the highest forms of spiritual pleasure and
that elementary one, quite without any social connotations, felt by
our lonely shepherds on the hills when they couple with their own
goats; if the comparison disgusts you that is because you are inca-
pable of making the necessary transposition from the bestial to the
superhuman planes, in my case superimposed on each other."

What the song of the Sirens had offered Odysseus when he
plied this bay was *knowledge*—"No life on earth can be / Hid from

our dreaming," they sang to him—and Lampedusa's Professor, like Odysseus, would seem to have gained knowledge complete, to know, in an ecstatic reunion of bestial and superhuman pleasures, all that the Sirens know: "Not for nothing," writes Lampedusa, is Lighea "the daughter of Calliope: ignorant of all culture, unaware of all wisdom, contemptuous of any moral inhibitions, she belonged, even so, to the fountainhead of all culture, of all wisdom, of all ethics, and could express this primitive superiority of hers in terms of rugged beauty. . . . That lascivious girl, that cruel wild beast, had also been a Wise Mother who, by her mere presence, had uprooted faiths, dissipated metaphysics." By having himself tied to the mast, and blocking up his men's ears with beeswax, cunning Odysseus gained all this, a knowledge before and after merely human knowledge. The Professor is not so lucky, or so clever, or maybe he just doesn't want to be Odyssean: "Certainly I shall not be the second man to disobey her call. I will not refuse that kind of pagan Grace that has been conceded me." With the whole truth of the ancients singing in his vitals, he resolves to join his Siren in the depths. As the liner *Rex* steams toward Naples, he disappears into the waters off Siren Land. Lifeboats are immediately launched. But no trace of the old Professor is found.

Douglas made nearly as elegant a departure. I enjoy, in the early evenings, climbing up to where it happened. Monte Tuoro is a forested hill ringed in terraces by the prettiest villas on the island. It was in one of these, owned by his friend Kenneth Macpherson, that Norman Douglas, incurably ill, took his life in February of 1952. "God be with you, my dears. You keep the Old Bugger. I shan't need Him," were his last volitional words. But as he lay comatose, Uncle Norman said "love" three times: once (I like to think) for those who'd been good to him, once for himself, and once for vanished realms carried within.

On Capri, the best evening pleasure is a walk to the Arco Naturale, freestanding mouth of what must have been a huge grotto like others pocking the island, then dinner outdoors at Le Grottelle, with its view of both slopes of the Sorrentine Peninsula, the lights of the southern coast brightening in the dusk: Positano, Praiano, Amalfi. Across the water, on a clear night, even a few glimmers of Salerno. In summer, a steady stream of cruise ships leave Sorrento for the overnight journey to Sicily. Capri, from their view, must present a fine aspect; the flashing of cameras never lets up. But tonight I want only to contemplate the peninsula yonder, specifically its headland, sacred in antiquity to Athena and the locale of that sixth-century-B.C. temple of which no trace remains. I have spent the past few afternoons over there; pretending to be Norman Douglas, I've scoured the place, at risk of life and limb, and come back each evening none the wiser.

"There really was a temple to Athena over there?" I ask Shirley, with whom I'm having dinner at Le Grottelle.

"We needn't doubt it. Strabo and others speak of an Athenaion or temple to Minerva, whether there on that flat bit, where you'd expect it to have been, or at the summit of Monte San Costanzo, or somewhere else nearby. But a Doric temple doesn't disappear without trace. All kinds of fragments have been unearthed from later periods on the headland, yet no evidences of a temple, on dry land or the surrounding sea floor. In the mid-1980s, however, something fascinating came to light—a large inscription, down under the lighthouse, on the rock face. About a meter high and three meters long. You wonder how it went unnoticed for centuries on end. It's in Oscan, written from right to left, and says, 'This is the way to ascend to the temple of Minerva,' and includes the names of several keepers of the place. The sunlight has to hit the crag just right for any of this to be visible. I suspect fishermen have noted it immemorially and not much cared."

"What's Oscan?" I ask, happy in such company to be the idiot questioner.

"An ancient language brought down from the Apennines and spoken here alongside Greek and Latin. The Campanian littoral has always been polyglot. We know that Oscan was still in use at Pompeii as late as the first century. Anyhow, between Greek and Roman rule came the Samnites, who introduced their language and ruled here for a couple of centuries, evidently assimilating Athena—Minerva—to their worship. But they were fierce enemies to Greeks and Romans both. And gave aid and comfort to Hannibal in the Second Punic War, for which they were not forgiven. History after that hears no more of the Samnites." (The inscription cannot be seen from the headland, and is exceptionally hard to see from the water. The learned journals tell me it looks like this:

But I have yet to see for myself.)

Conversation like Shirley's takes you very far from touristic Capri: the meretricious lure of the Blue Grotto, the shops of via

Camerelle in which red plastic is passed off as coral, the floodtide of visitors inundating Marina Grande. Worst of all is the Quisisana. Visiting Capri some months after his release from Reading Gaol in 1897, Oscar Wilde and his ruinous great love, Lord Alfred "Bosie" Douglas, entered the Quisi dining room, whereupon the English clientele rose from their seats—in indignation, of course, not homage. Federico Serena, proprietor of the hotel and mayor of Capri, told Wilde and Bosie to leave. Eternal shame on the Quisi.

Ivan Bunin's short story "The Gentleman from San Francisco" tells of a wealthy American's fatal stay there. While perusing a newspaper, the gentleman from San Francisco suddenly starts to claw at his starched collar and shirtfront, writhing as if in a fight with himself. His pince-nez flies off, he lets out a violent wheeze. Such unpleasantness might well be hushed up by the management—a figure who is unmistakably Serena, proprietor of the Quisi, tries to assure his guests that it's nothing, nothing—but for a German who spreads the word that a death is under way. Bad night for the Quisi: "Many of those dining leapt up, many of them, turning pale, ran to the reading-room and 'What, what's happened?' was heard in every language—and no one could give an intelligible answer, no one understood anything, because even today people still marvel above all else at death and refuse to accept it." It's an extraordinary sentence, the "even today" worthy of Tolstoy or Chekhov, Bunin's masters. On the floor of the reading room his protagonist continues to writhe. With ebbing strength, he fights the enemy who has fallen on him, even as the deeply embarrassed management hurriedly pick him up and cart him off to "the smallest, nastiest, dampest and coldest room in the hotel, at the end of the bottom corridor." The first half of the story has made clear that this gentleman from San Francisco is about as loathsome a character as you could ever want to meet—arrogant, stupid, mean. Only there in room 43 does he come morally into his own, through the boundless humiliation of death.

So much for the Quisi. At the furthest emotional remove, perched dizzyingly above Marina Piccola on a crag of the Solaro, far from all but the most dedicated sightseer, is the little church of Santa Maria a Cetrella. Take the chairlift from Anacapri's central square, a twelve-minute thrill of a ride, to the summit; from there a rocky path and then a straight one lead across a valley to Capri's holiest, humblest, and purest embodiment of its native architectural traditions, a stuccoed, low-vaulted, primordially Franciscan chapel and hermitage, attached barnacle-like to the sheer drop. Rilke, no fan of this island, which already in 1906 he found rather trashy, was deeply moved by the portrait of the Virgin that pilgrims come here to venerate. And so they have for at least ten centuries. Santa Maria a Cetrella played the role in the Middle Ages that the temple to Minerva at Punta della Campanella had played in antiquity. The goddess gave succor to those in peril on the sea—especially Capri's coral fishermen, who sailed as far as Corsica and the North African coast, braving not just the weather but, as fearsome, Barbary pirates trafficking in Christian flesh. Capriote youths sailed out of the marinas and never saw home again, sold at market as they routinely were for labor in North Africa or the Levant, or as galley oarsmen for infidel ships. Intercession by the Holy Mother of Cetrella was the island's best hope against such terrifying possibilities, and she was propitiated annually at a Festa della Madonna di Cetrella with prayers and ex votos, some of which are set into the interior walls here: a model ship, a fragment of what looks like an oar, each the bearer of a story, whether of hope for safe return or of grief for men lost. It is said that the generations of hermits who kept the shrine—the last of their line died in 1889; his initials are carved into a stone at the entrance to one room—would light an oil lamp to signal to those sailing the waters south of Capri, assurance of the Madonna of Cetrella's protection.

If this is Capri's most otherworldly church, its worldliest is the Church of San Michele Arcangelo in Anacapri, with its fabulous majolica pavement. Completed in 1719, San Michele is the work of a leading architect, painter, and sculptor of the first half of the eighteenth century, Domenico Antonio Vaccaro. The floor, installed around the middle of the century, is the work of Leonardo Chiaiese, an artist from Abruzzo who brought his stupendous skills to Naples, where majolica was much favored, and produced at Anacapri this tremendous work in the medium. You may walk as slowly as you like all round the edge of the hourglass-shaped pavement, or else climb a spiral staircase to the choir loft for a view of the whole. But really there is no view of the whole. It's too big and intricate; the eye gets lost in details. At the midmost, Adam and Eve are ordered from paradise by a sword-bearing angel on a cloud. A compliant Adam flings out his arms in the direction of the wilderness, the world, history. Eve beseeches the angel one last time. Before them, in the lower, lesser part of the hourglass, where trees are bent and broken and unbeautiful, is the world as we know it. Oxen and goats and rams are there, the animals domesticated to human use, who gaze back with startlingly human eyes; also a unicorn; and the she-wolf of the Palatine, growling at Romulus as he reaches for a teat. The fallen realms of nature, then, along with those of pagan myth. But behind Adam and Eve is all that God created before His handiwork included them (and He saw that it was not just good but very good): a limpid, starry, moonlit, cloud-dappled sky, and under that, the broad day with sun ablaze; and beasts familiar and strange, including, in pairs mostly, ostriches, badgers, curly-tailed dogs, peacocks, a thing that seems half raccoon and half porcupine, house cats, leopards, a solitary turkey, an alligator alone on the bank (whose mate may be shyly underwater), dromedaries, mice, a depressed-looking elephant. And against the two horizon lines, one dividing the firmament into day and night, the other marking off land from water, stands the Tree of Knowledge, dense with fruit and girt round with the Serpent.

And yet, and yet—an allegorical owl perches on one bough, as much as to say that this tree is not just of damning knowledge but of redeeming wisdom. (I cannot be alone in having observed, faint but demonstrably there, the view of the Bay that one has from Capri on a clear morning: from left to right, Capo Miseno, the Posillipo headland, Camaldoli, Vesuvius.) Those worshipping here at San Michele may or may not have known the legend of the True Cross, which claims that as 930-year-old Adam lay dying, Seth, the son of his old age, hurried to the gates of Heaven to ask the Archangel Michael for some oil of the wood of mercy with which to save his father. The archangel refused Seth, saying that there could be no mercy for another five thousand years, till the sacrifice of Christ on the Cross. Michael gave him, instead, a limb from this Tree of Good and Evil—the one on which Chiaiese's owl sits—and told Seth that when that branch had grown into a tree and that tree had borne fruit, then Adam could be saved. Seth placed the branch in his dead father's mouth and from it a new tree grew. In the fullness of time, says the Apocrypha, this tree was cut down to make the cross on which Christ was crucified. In other words, while the first fruit of that tree expelled us from Eden into history, the final fruit, Christ's sacrifice on the cross, has granted us daughters and sons of Adam redemption, second innocence, life everlasting, our way back to the garden.

Look all you want at Chiaiese's depiction of that paradise, but the only fruit-bearing tree you will find there is the forbidden one. So what choice, in this blue and green and gold majolica world, did our first parents have but to learn everything and grow wise? What other food was there but knowledge? Chiaiese's pavement is a humanistic triumph.

CONCLUSION

Lacrimae Rerum

*Happy the much-traveled foreigner, who comes and leaves,
sated with impressions, which are turned into judgments and,
eventually, into nostalgia.*

—Susan Sontag, *The Volcano Lover*

*T*he comprehensive hell of 1939–1945 is greater by orders of magnitude than books can contain. The more you examine the record, the more you wonder what possible infamy was *not* perpetrated in those six years. And, as if by a reversal of perspective, the Second World War seems to grow vaster as it recedes. Particular writers have dwelled on particular monstrosities to stand for the whole. Thus, for example, in his great lecture "The Human Condition," Camus tells of the Greek mother forced by Waffen-SS to choose one of her three sons to be spared execution. She could not, says Camus, "convince the German officer that it was not seemly for him to arrange her heartbreak. For S. S. men and German officers were no longer men, representing men, but like an instinct elevated to the height of an idea or a theory. Passion, even if murderous, would have been less evil." Even the darkness of the Dark Ages does not compare, Camus argues, as the modern instrumentalities of Nazi murder, along with the modern ideological rationalizations for such ineffable crimes, changed the nature of the inhumanity. Regarding the Second World War, one is left always with the imponderable supplement to recorded agony, the enormities not in the historical record, vast though it is, for 1939–1945 were years in which the versatility of evil knew its widest fulfillment.

Mussolini had entered the maelstrom on June 11, 1940, confident of linking his North African colonial possessions with those in the Horn of Africa by conquering Egypt, thereby to lay claim to the Suez Canal and the vast oilfields of Arabia: fit imperium for a man who saw himself as the modern world's answer to Augustus. Imagining that the course of Italy's engagement in the conflict would be as auspicious as the acquisition of Libya, war in Ethiopia, and annexation of Albania had proven, the Duce was in high spirits when in October 1940 he invaded Greece. Flush with his Ethiopian successes, he'd not been prepared to see Greek forces drive half a million Italian troops back into Albania. To counteract this, Hitler was forced to come to Mussolini's aid, committing men and matériel to a Balkan theater he'd not wished to open, invading first Yugoslavia and then Greece. The pacification of Greece, especially, would preoccupy him for six months, a distraction from his great hidden ambition, the conquest and abolition of the Soviet Union. That operation commenced only on June 22, three weeks after the fall of Crete. Buoyed by the Red Army's poor showing a year earlier against the Finns, whom they outnumbered tremendously and yet could not subdue, Hitler had imagined his campaign against the Soviet Union would succeed within a matter of months ("You have only to kick in the door and the whole rotten structure will come crashing down," he said). The consequences of that miscalculation, culminating in the snows of Stalingrad, would cost him the war.

Ordinary Italians felt no special enmity for any of the Reich's opponents—France and Great Britain, latterly the Soviet Union and the United States. Mussolini's plunge into the conflict would quickly diminish his popularity with them. Military reversals in North Africa mounted despite Field Marshal Rommel's presence. In the three years of Italy's involvement, more than 350,000 soldiers would surrender to British and American forces: in the Horn of Africa in 1941, in Libya in 1941–1943, in Tunisia in 1943. Add to that the sacrifice of Italy's entire Eighth Army—220,000 men—at Stalingrad, and you begin to get the sense of how utterly calamitous the Duce's adventure proved to be for his people. In the light of such losses, and after the Allied conquest of Sicily, the Italian high command, whose ultimate loyalty was to the House of Savoy, demanded his resignation. Hitler was enraged though scarcely surprised when, on September 8, 1943, Italy agreed to an armistice with the United States and Great Britain. Marshal Pietro Badoglio, Mussolini's successor, appointed by King Vittorio Emanuele III, declared in a radio broadcast: "The Italian government, recognizing the impossibility of continuing the unequal struggle against an overwhelming enemy force, in order to avoid further and graver disasters for the Nation, sought an armistice from General Eisenhower, commander-in-chief of the Anglo-American Allied forces. The request was granted. Consequently, all acts of hostility against the Anglo-American force by Italian forces must cease everywhere. But they may react to eventual attacks from any other source." Thus the stage was set for nineteen bloody months of war between the German army and the Italian people.

But back in the summer of 1941, with Axis hopes at their peak and Operation Barbarossa (as the German invasion of the USSR, the largest military operation in human history, was code-named) only three weeks old, Mussolini assessed the bombings of the vitally strategic port of Naples and, doubtless imagining Italy and Germany to be invincible and total victory imminent, took a philosophical view of the disasters of war, saying to his son-in-law and heir apparent, Count Ciano: "I'm delighted that Naples is suffering. These dreadful nights will toughen the Southern race. This war will make Northerners of them." Mussolini had but two years left in power when he said this, and less than four to live. Naples would be bombed repeatedly in these years, suffering more damage and a larger number of casualties, as I say, than any other Italian city.

Nineteen forty-three was the culmination. In March, the explosion of an Italian armament ship in port killed hundreds at the quayside and maimed many more. In July, a massive Allied bombardment killed three thousand Neapolitans and injured thousands more. After Badoglio's September proclamation, joyful shouts of

Viva Napoli Liberata, *October 1943*

"La guerra è finita!" were heard from the Vomero to the Sanità. But Italy's war with its former German ally, and with the remaining Fascist militias, had only just begun.

In the final three weeks of German occupation of Naples, following Italian surrender, one spectacle of peculiar savagery seems to have galvanized active resistance. A thousand Neapolitans were herded at gunpoint into the stretch of the Rettifilo facing the university to witness the burning of the library, and were ordered to kneel and applaud the execution of an Italian sailor. That same day, another five hundred citizens were conducted to Teverola, in the Casertano, and forced to witness the execution of thirteen *carabinieri* accused of resisting German orders. Then, on September 23, Colonel Walter Schöll, the ranking German official at Naples, suddenly ordered the evacuation of everyone living up to three hundred meters inland from the sea; 240,000 souls were commandeered at short notice from homes they had every reason to believe were about to be destroyed.

The breaking point came several days later, when posters appeared throughout the city ordering all males between the ages of eighteen and thirty-three to report for "voluntary service within the Reich," i.e., deportation for slave labor. Schöll expected thirty thousand able-bodied men to turn up; only one hundred fifty did so. At that point, a new decree over his name announced that noncompliance with the "voluntary service" order would be punished by summary execution. Popular insurrection was then inevitable.

Hitler ordered Schöll to reduce Naples "to mud and ashes"— perhaps a knowing reference to Herculaneum and Pompeii?— before the retreat. It was an instruction that could not have been carried out in any case. Harried as they were by the newly formed resistance fighters—among them young street boys, or *scugnizzi*—it was all the Germans could do to get themselves to Salerno, where Allied forces had just landed, and from there to the Gustav Line and Monte Cassino, where Hitler hoped to halt the Allied advance. The last ninety-six hours of German occupation, September 27–30,

1943, have entered Neapolitan history as the Quattro Giornate. What actually happened in the streets of the Sanità and the Quartieri Spagnoli and on the Vomero belongs as much to myth as to fact, and the two are by now not entirely separable. Afterward, those taking part either wished not to speak about what they'd done—or else were too eager, handing journalists and historians the jazzed-up lore they thought was wanted. But what is beyond question is that at Naples, in the course of those four great days, citizen fighters mounted the first successful urban insurrection against the Nazi war machine. When Allied forces entered the city at nine-thirty a.m. on October 1, Germans (at least living ones) were nowhere to be found.

Naples was a place the Reich had thoroughly learned to hate. On the last day of Schöll's occupation, a final outrage was perpetrated. Nearby, at Villa Montesano, in the village of San Paolo Belsito, irreplaceable documents of the Neapolitan State Archives had been deposited for safekeeping. Departing Germans, aware of the value of this vast patrimony, set fire to it. What perished in the flames were all documents pertaining to the years 1265 to 1505—which is

to say, all of the historical records of Angevin and Aragonese Naples, along with still earlier papers dating from the reign of Frederick II, along with extensive papers from the Spanish and Bourbon centuries. After so many German initiatives against flesh and blood came this final gesture, against intellect—this bonfire of the Neapolitan past.

In Curzio Malaparte's novel-memoir *La pelle* (*The Skin*), published in 1949, a good deal of otherwise unavailable documentary

Neapolitan news vendor,
November 1943

evidence of the *giornate* is preserved: "The boys and women were most to be dreaded during those four days of strife, in which no quarter was asked or given. I myself saw the corpses of many German soldiers, still unburied two days after the liberation, with lacerated faces and throats mangled by human teeth. Many had been disfigured by scissors. Many lay in pools of blood with long nails driven into their skulls. For lack of other weapons the boys had driven those long nails into the Germans' heads with large stones while ten or twenty enraged lads held them on the ground." These details are factual, whatever else in Malaparte's work is not. As with *Kaputt*, his earlier book about the war, there is in *The Skin* a shuttling between reportage and phantasmagoria. At his worst, Malaparte was a self-propagandist predisposed to half-truths announced in overheated rhetoric. First an ardent Fascist, then a convinced Stalinist, afterward an enthusiastic Maoist, and finally, when he knew he was dying, a devout Roman Catholic, he adopted these postures in opportunistic ways as the occasion suited, becoming whatever the weather called for. "An intellectual harlequin and consummate arriviste," as Dan Hofstadter has accurately written.

Add to this his slavering, obsessive hatred of "inverts," which in *The Skin* leads him to claim that homosexuality caused the Second World War. A man who can argue that can argue anything. Yet in the dubious bravura of his prose is also brilliance, and information otherwise lost about the Allied occupation, when Naples sought "to win at the side of the Allies the same war we had already lost at the side of the Germans." When he tells of GIs who, sated on other pleasures, pay money to see an intact virgin, one senses he is reporting a fact: "The girl threw her cigarette on the floor, grasped the fringe of her petticoat with the tips of her fingers and slowly raised it. First

her knees appeared, gently gripped by the silk sheath of her stock-
ings, then the bare skin of her thighs. She remained for a moment
in this posture, a sad Veronica, her face severe, her mouth half-open
in an expression of contempt. Then, slowly turning on her back,
she lay at full length on the bed." Her pimp, if that's the word for
him—her manager, let's say—thrusts his head through a curtained
door to say, "You can touch. Don't be afraid."

When Malaparte describes black marketeers pilfering goods
from a Liberty ship in the harbor, I certainly believe him. When he
goes on to claim they stole the ship too, I have my doubts, extravagantly charming though the prose is: "It vanished, and was never
heard of again. All Naples, from Capodimonte to Posillipo, rocked
with tumultuous laughter, as if convulsed by an earthquake. The
Muses, the Graces, Juno, Minerva, Diana and all the Goddesses
from Olympus, who in the cool of the evening appear in the clouds
above Vesuvius and look down on Naples, could be seen laughing
and clasping their bosoms with both hands, while Venus made the
heavens shimmer with the flashing of her white teeth."

Alan Moorehead, Australian-born correspondent for the London *Daily Express*, conscientious and precise where Malaparte is

Neapolitans warming themselves, circa 1944

flamboyant and out to shock, makes
a useful contrast; and comes out
ahead. Anticipating, on his arrival
with the British, an angry or sul-
len greeting from Neapolitans, he
found instead only animal hunger
and rampaging typhus: "In tens of
thousands the dirty ragged children
kept crying for biscuits and sweets.

When we stopped the jeep we were immediately surrounded and overwhelmed. Thrusting hands picked at our clothing. *Pane. Biscotti. Sigarette.* In every direction there was a wall of emaciated, hungry, dirty faces." Stolen *sigarette* and *caramelle* were the de facto currency. Six-year-old boys hawked pornographic postcards, or their sisters, or themselves, or led you to a hellhole featuring acts between children and animals. Moorehead reports on a night sortie of the Luftwaffe over Naples harbor, American and British ships answering with tracer fire as the German bombers dove in and out of the searchlights and the barrage, while in the background Vesuvius flashed and smoldered. He reports also on the lightning spread of a resistant strain of gonorrhea among Allied soldiers. Roads into the city were duly posted with warnings of the epidemic, but young men under arms are young men. "Several hundred new cases were reported every week, and before Christmas we were taking more casualties in Naples through gonorrhea than through enemy action on the whole of the front-line."

Meanwhile, he notes, through the long years of war Capri had remained its old self: "The horse with the nodding plumes to run you up to Anacapri or down to the Piccola Marina. The Quisisana. The Funicular. It was as though someone had placed a glass bowl over the whole confection in 1939, and now that the bowl was lifted again the people came out, a little jaded, like a railway sandwich, but quite genuine Capri stock." It had been the favored retreat of German officers and Fascist higher-ups till the collapse.

My modus operandi has been to walk a knowledge of Naples into my bloodstream. Even under pummeling August suns, when the city shrinks behind closed shutters and the streets and squares are blasted with light, I have shunned buses, subways, taxis, harrowing though it can be to cross some of these byways on foot. (A worldly English friend, a connoisseur of taxicabs, tells me she prefers Neapolitan drivers to those of any other city. "As handsome as movie stars," she says. "As learned as Coleridge. And gallant, to boot." Well, my friend is a beautiful woman. People are glad to see her.)

One airless evening, I lose heart and step into an exquisitely air-conditioned cab. The olive-skinned movie star at the wheel flourishes a set of perfect teeth and asks my destination. Don't have one, I realize. "Capodimonte," I propose. "Could you take the longest way?" On his dashboard is a library: back issues of *Il mattino*, a Tom Clancy in Italian, Aldous Huxley's *La filosofia perenne*, a couple of books on Buddhism.

"Buddhism," I say. "Is it true that Buddhism is atheistic?"

"Sono novizio, signore. È una domanda troppo difficile per me." I'm a novice, sir. That's too difficult a question for me.

"I'm Ben."

"Mi chiamo Edo." Edo proceeds to the Four Noble Truths. According to the Dharmacakra Pravartana Sutra, life is suffering, or *dukkha*. The sources of *dukkha* are appetite, ego, I-me-mine-ism. The way out of suffering is the escape from egocentrism. So far, so good. But expounding the fourth truth, which branches into eight additional truths, he loses me in a maze of hard-to-follow Italian. Still, if this much-branching Fourth Noble Truth unriddles life's riddle, I need to get it straight. Or else I'm just being polite; when people start talking about the One and Nirvana and Perennial Philosophies—honestly, I fade out. Edo believes in transcendence.

All I've got is history: origin and course of things, growth and decay, fates of cities. Yet between him, devoted to Siddhartha Gautama, and me, descended from Francis Bacon and G. B. Vico, I sense there is going to be plenty to talk about. I propose a bite of dinner at a nameless dive outside the Capodimonte museum gates. Such a dinner might be socially unusual in London or Paris; I know it would be so in New York. But this is Naples, where life readily takes such turns.

We place our orders at the counter, then grab a free table. Beers and pizzas before us, Edo tells how Gautama sat under the Bodhi Tree and awaited enlightenment for forty-nine days.

"I know what he found out, Edo. That selfhood and self-seeking are the cause of all suffering. So self is what we are meant to escape. But selves are what this human stuff is packaged into. We're *condannati* in the prison house of the self. What's that word you have in Italian for 'life without parole'?"

"*Ergastolo.*"

"*Ergastolo.* That's my truth, as surely as Nirvana is yours. And what's to regret? Relinquishing selfhood sounds to me like death. I know some manage to see it as reunion with the One. I see it as just plain death, the Great Adversary. I'm a writer and live among writers, the extravagantly talented and the sort of talented both, and I've never met one who wanted out of selfhood. Selfhood's their magic cabinet. Every one of them believes himself or herself to be inwardly full of wonders, wonders it would be a calamity for humankind to do without."

"*Pericoloso, questo atteggiamento.*" Dangerous attitude, that.

"You said it. *Morally* dangerous to see yourself in that light. But egocentrism, well or poorly managed, is the writer's fate. 'No end to the vanity of our calling,' as a great English poet said." We sit awhile in silence, Edo content to let me have the last word, maybe sensing I need it, as always. (Not my best trait. No end to the vanity.) But now I watch something happen on his face. The Buddhistic serenity fades away and a bright-eyed young man's appetites are there instead.

"I think something very good may be about to happen," he says. "I mean, happen to *me*."

"To you? To the *self* called you?"

"To me."

"Let me guess. You've . . . met someone."

"*Esatto.*"

"Okay, tell."

"*È bellissima.*"

"Of course she is. *Complimenti, Edo.*"

"*Intelligente, colta, raffinata.*"

"*Auguri, Edo.* Where'd you meet her?"

"In my taxi."

"Oh."

"*Ieri.*"

"Oh." Evergreen hope, glory of youth. "You got her number, I trust."

"No, but she will be in Naples for the week. *Americana.* From the city of South Orange. You have heard of it?"

"I have, yes. Do you at least know her hotel, Edo?"

"No, but I will look for her in the likely places—the Gambrinus, the Museo Archeologico, at Santa Lucia."

Napoletanissimo, I say to myself. Quintessentially Neapolitan. And he probably *will* find her. "Edo, did you ever see a French picture called *Children of Paradise*?" I ask. "In it, a man says to a beautiful woman named Garance, 'But how will I find you? Paris is big.' And Garance says, 'For those who love as we do, Paris is small!' For those who love as you do, Edo, Naples is small. You'll find your South Orange Garance."

He spontaneously leans across the table and gives me two kisses. I do get a kick out of these guys—so heterosexual, but who so help-lessly prefer the company of their own sex. You see it in the way the youths here cluster together. Grown men are the same. Observing all their kissing and hand-holding, visitors have imagined Naples to be a hotbed of homosexual activity, which it is not. The ardor is from the neck up. "After dinner, I am making you a gift," Edo says. "We turn off the meter of the taxi and I drive you to Camaldoli. You have been?" Camaldoli is the big mountain behind Naples, domi-nated by a monastery. "At night," says Edo, "you can see all the way to Gaeta, if the weather is fine. My brother used to tell me it was Rome, and I believed him."

So up we go, getting better acquainted en route. At the men-tion of family, I am pierced by home-thoughts—if not as miserably as another American in Naples, Lucky Luciano, leading gangster of his generation, forced to stay on here after the war. Despite numer-ous services to the American occupying army, he had not been allowed to return to the States. Poor Lucky was homesickness itself. He would haunt Ristorante California, down at Santa Lucia quay, consoling himself with a bowl of Texas-style chili or fried chicken and waffles or peach cobbler à la mode, any old-country treat.

*Lucky Luciano in exile,
circa 1955*

Hearing American English at a nearby table, he'd go over, modestly introduce himself, and pull up a chair to have a chat. How he loved it when autograph hounds from Kansas City or Sheboygan would show up at his medical-supply store, a front for myriad criminal enterprises. One day in 1962, after lunch, Lucky dropped dead. People speculated that he'd been poisoned. But if homesickness can kill, Luciano died of it.

Edo and I are admiring the view from the Belvedere Camaldoli. Naples is spread out, indeed like an antique map, before us. The panorama is dotted with various fireworks displays, usually signifying a wedding, but also, tonight, with garbage fires. If Shanghai and Delhi and Cairo can manage their waste disposal, why not Naples? Because the refuse industry is controlled by the Camorra. In a demonstration of power, these gangsters periodically halt collection. Garbage accumulates in monumental piles all over town, producing in summer a crazy-making stench. When people get crazy enough, they set fire to the piles, and this is what is happening tonight.

Someone said, long ago, that Europe ends at Naples, and ends badly. I guess it does. The vermin have won, someone said more recently. I guess they have. Two mornings ago when I stepped out onto my little balcony for a look at the growing hillock across the street, I saw a rat cross quite calmly, root around in the filth, then emerge triumphant with—no, what in God's name was that, held between needle teeth? I raced downstairs and asked the porter whether he'd seen. "A human hand!" I hollered.

"*Si calmi, Signor Taylor, per carità. Non era che una costoletta.*" A cutlet, he thinks he saw. He calls to the doorman one building down, "*Marco, hai visto quella stronza? Che cosa strascinava?*" Marco, you saw that piece of shit? What was she dragging?

"*Quella sgualdrina? Sì, l'ho vista. Strascinava un pezzo di pesce spada.*" That tramp? Yeah, I saw her. A piece of swordfish, she was dragging.

Edo grew up in the Quartieri Spagnoli, he tells me, in a little family. "Only my older brother and our parents. Our father died when I was fifteen. Well, fathers were dying all over the Quartieri at about the age of fifty, fifty-five. While eating or arguing or chasing tail." (He's slipped back into Italian; I am translating.) "I wasn't unprepared. I'd come to regard grown men as frail beings. Women, on the other hand, I saw as indestructible. Last night they showed *Roma città aperta* on TV. Did you see it? There's this scene where Anna Magnani is running after the truck that's carrying off her fiancé. And one of the *fascisti* in the truck shoots her. Just shoots her in the road. I do not know why, but I think it's the most terrible thing I've ever seen in a film."

"*Open City*. Has the true *terribilità*, no? A word we have no equivalent for in English. None of the other women die in the picture, as I remember. Yes, next to the men they really do seem indestructible, more part of nature. So when one of them gets shot dead it seems out of the order of things, even though such abominations are happening all around. But your mother. Your mother after your father died."

"She sank. She stopped talking. Her face turned a yellowish gray and stayed like that. She took up smoking, which shocked my brother and me. She'd always been against it. Used to make Babbo go into the street to smoke. Many tirades at our house."

"You lost her?"

"My brother Valentino got mixed up with *gente cattiva*." I understood the euphemism. People here often use it instead of saying Camorristi straight-out. *Gente cattiva*: wicked people, a term covering everyone from the most invisible international bosses to the lowliest local foot soldiers. Having survived so many dominations over the millennia, Naples now has the Camorra to survive. "He was spending time at Le Vele, in Scampia, visiting friends in the high-rises." These were miracles of low-cost housing built in the seventies and eighties. They have degenerated into Camorra-controlled open-air drug markets with more than sixty percent of the population unemployed and a criminal hierarchy inducting *ragazzini* as young as eight and nine. (The brutality and unpredictability of life in Le Vele has been unforgettably documented by Roberto Saviano in his entirely nonfictional "novel" *Gomorrah*, and dramatized by Matteo Garrone in the film adaptation of Saviano's book.)

I know what is coming next, know Valentino is dead one way or another in the jungles of the northern *periferia*, where as if by an iron law somebody must die of an overdose or a gunshot wound every day.

"But your mother?"

"About eighteen months after Valentino she—"

And suddenly the water is coming down my face too, for selfish reasons, as I have lost a family of my own while writing this book: brother, father, mother, one after the other, I explain. Three boulders thrust into my arms, to carry as best I can. But I didn't know how heavy they'd get. Alike in bereavement, Edo and I sit awhile, not hurrying our tears. Mine come freely. His are slower, more glycerine-like. A voice within tells me to keep, whatever else I may lose, this evening, this hour, this moment. This.

Memory bestows everything; nostalgia bestows nothing. Nostalgia is but a prettified fragment of a fragment. Memory keeps hold of the discrepant, the ugly, the unbearable. Remember these, I tell myself: the rat, the stench, the citywide toxic fires, the broken-hearted son and brother. Let these be your vaccination against nostalgia. And then an image great in *terribilità* rises up: Jusepe de Ribera's *Prometheus,* painted at Naples in the 1630s—a figure wildly contorted, fastened by Zeus to a boulder, visited daily by an eagle who feeds on his liver. It is executed in the dramatically tenebrist and naturalistic style that Lo Spagnoletto ("The Little Spaniard," as Ribera was known here) had learned from Caravaggio. For wronging the new gods, this old god, or Titan, must anguish for aeons, liver growing anew overnight only to be eaten again next day by the ravening bird. Prometheus's sins? Saving humankind from destruction by Zeus and, beyond that, conferring fire, agriculture, animal husbandry, metallurgy, navigation, alphabets, time-telling, carpentry, architecture, mathematics, and astronomy. Writing twenty-five hundred years ago, when Neapolis was new, Aeschylus adds in his *Prometheus Bound* that Prometheus conferred, beyond all these practical blessings, the most human-making one of all: the vitalizing ignorance of how and when each of us shall die, the merciful mystery of things to come:

> *Prometheus:*
> I caused mortals to cease foreseeing doom.

> *Chorus:*
> What cure did you provide them with against that sickness?

> *Prometheus:*
> I placed in them blind hopes.

> *Chorus:*
> That was a great gift you gave to men.

I keep coming back to Ribera's picture. Prometheus, greatest of benefactors, writhes in his manacles as the eagle swoops stupidly to feed from his gashed-open flank. Fair enough, I think—a just metaphor for the *napoletanità* I've struggled these years to lay hold of, always despairing. A city where so much has been felt and thought and made, so much contributed to the sum of glorious and curious human things. But a city that has suffered so, and whose disproportionate agony is ongoing. Heroic in unequal combat, battered, degraded, ruined. Yet titanic. Not so much a Christ as a Prometheus among cities. That is what Naples declared to me.

ACKNOWLEDGMENTS

In the interest of privacy, certain names and details have been changed. This is a book of memory and reflection, not reportage. Over the course of sixteen years, during eleven stays in Naples, I talked to hundreds of people; nobody, however, was "interviewed" for these pages. I took only sketchy notes, and none in line with good journalistic practice. What I did instead, year after year, was to let the interesting, sometimes funny or poignant things learned from near-strangers settle down in me, and only now have I made the inventory.

Without Irene Skolnick, I could not have begun. Without Marian Wood, I could not have seen my way. Without Patrick Callihan, I could not have mastered the disorder. Without John Reynolds, I would not have come through. Warm thanks are owed also to Ivan Held Alaina Mauro, Susan Walsh, Amanda Dewey, and Anna Jardine. Both the Corporation of Yaddo and The MacDowell Colony gave me shelter. Joel Conarroe, Patricia Volk, Nick Barberio, Daphne Merkin, Alison West, Frances and Howard Kiernan, Stephen Motika, and David Goodwillie helped immensely with faith and works. My friendship with Leonard Barkan opened the treasure house of art history. Dr. Joseph Rudick gave me new eyes to see with. Someone I do not name taught me to work harder.

SOURCES

Though a walk is a walk and not a work of scholarship, I owe frequent debts in these pages to very many learned sources. Happy nights and days were spent with the following:

Allanbrook, Douglas. *See Naples: A Memoir*. Boston: Houghton Mifflin, 1995.

Astarita, Tommaso. *Between Salt Water and Holy Water: A History of Southern Italy*. New York: W. W. Norton, 2005.

Belmonte, Thomas. *The Broken Fountain*. New York: Columbia University Press, 1979.

Boardman, John, Jasper Griffin, and Oswyn Murray, eds. *The Oxford Illustrated History of Greece and the Hellenistic World*. Oxford and New York: Oxford University Press, 1986.

———, eds. *The Oxford Illustrated History of Rome*. Oxford and New York: Oxford University Press, 1986.

Brunschwig, Jacques, and Geoffrey E. R. Lloyd, eds. *The Greek Pursuit of Knowledge*. Trans. under the direction of Catherine Porter. Cambridge, Mass.: The Belknap Press of Harvard University Press, 2000.

———, eds. *A Guide to Greek Thought: Major Figures and Trends*. Trans. under the direction of Catherine Porter. Cambridge, Mass.: The Belknap Press of Harvard University Press, 2000.

Croce, Benedetto. *History of the Kingdom of Naples*. Ed. H. Stuart Hughes, trans. Frances Frenaye. Chicago: University of Chicago

Press, 1970. Originally published as *Storia del regno di Napoli*. Bari: Laterza, 1925.

———. *Storie e leggende napoletane*. Ed. Giuseppe Galasso. Milan: Adelphi, 1990.

de Jorio, Andrea. *Gesture in Naples and Gesture in Classical Antiquity*. Trans. and with introduction and notes by Adam Kendon. Bloomington: Indiana University Press, 2000. Originally published as *La mimica degli antichi investigata nel gestire napoletano*. Naples: Stamperia e Carteria del Fibreno, 1832.

Finley, M. I. *The World of Odysseus*. New York: New York Review Books, 2002.

———, ed. *The Legacy of Greece: A New Appraisal*. Oxford and New York: Oxford University Press, 1981.

Ghirelli, Antonio. *Storia di Napoli*. Milan: Einaudi, 1992.

Gibbon, Edward. *The Decline and Fall of the Roman Empire*. New York: Alfred A. Knopf, 1993.

Gleijeses, Vittorio. *Storia di Napoli: Dalle origini ai nostri giorni*. Naples: Società Editrice Napoletana, 1974.

Goethe, Johann Wolfgang von. *Italian Journey*. Trans. W. H. Auden and Elizabeth Mayer. New York: Pantheon, 1962.

Grafton, Anthony, Glen W. Most, and Salvatore Settis, eds. *The Classical Tradition*. Cambridge, Mass.: Harvard University Press, 2010.

Gunn, Peter. *Naples: A Palimpsest*. London: Chapman & Hall, 1961.

Hare, Augustus J. C. *Cities of Southern Italy and Sicily*. London: Smith, Elder, 1883.

Hazzard, Shirley, and Francis Steegmuller. *The Ancient Shore: Dispatches from Naples*. Chicago: University of Chicago Press, 2008.

Hofstadter, Dan. *Falling Palace: A Romance of Naples*. New York: Alfred A. Knopf, 2005.

Hutton, Edward. *Naples and Campania Revisited*. London: Hollis & Carter, 1958.

Lancaster, Jordan. *In the Shadow of Vesuvius: A Cultural History of Naples*. London: I. B. Tauris, 2005.

Liccardo, Giovanni. *Guida insolita ai misteri, ai segreti, alle leggende e alle curiosità di Napoli sotterranea*. Rome: Newton & Compton, 2000.

Matthews, Jeff. Around Naples Encyclopedia (website). http://acsupport.europe.umuc.edu/~jmatthew/naples/newAN.html.

Crockery merchant, 1947

Moe, Nelson. *The View from Vesuvius: Italian Culture and the Southern Question*. Berkeley: University of California Press, 2002.

Morton, H. V. *A Traveller in Southern Italy*. New York: Dodd, Mead, 1969.

Musto, Ronald G., general ed. *A Documentary History of Naples*. New York: Italica Press.

Napoli e dintorni: Guida d'Italia del Touring Club Italiano, 5th ed. Milan: Touring Club Italiano, 1976.

Napoli nobilissima: Rivista di arti figurative, archeologia e urbanistica.

Ramage, Craufurd Tait. *Ramage in South Italy: The Nooks and By-Ways of Italy: Wanderings in Search of Its Ancient Remains and Modern Superstitions*. Ed. Edith Clay. London: Longmans, Green, 1965.

Robb, Peter. *Street Fight in Naples: A Book of Art and Insurrection*. Sydney: Allen & Unwin, 2010.

Storia di Napoli, vols. 1–11. Naples: Società Editrice Storia di Napoli, 1967–1978.

Intellectual debts within particular chapters are as follows:

Introduction: One Hundred Fifty Generations

For accounts of eighteenth- and nineteenth-century British travel to the Continent, I have turned to Christopher Hibbert, *The Grand Tour* (London: Weidenfeld & Nicolson, 1969). Walter Benjamin's "Naples" is in *Reflections: Essays, Aphorisms, Autobiographical Writings*, edited by Peter Demetz, translated by Edmund Jephcott (New York: Harcourt, Brace, Jovanovich, 1978). Details of Leopardi's life are owed to Iris Origo, *Leopardi: A Study in Solitude* (London: Hamish Hamilton, 1953). Like all anglophone readers, I am indebted to the translations of Leopardi by Jonathan Galassi, and to his introduction to *Canti* (New York: Farrar, Straus & Giroux, 2010). I have quoted from Galassi's version of "Dello Stesso," the final poem of the volume.

One. From Pithekoussai

I have quoted from *Arturo's Island* (New York: Alfred A. Knopf, 1959), Isabel Quigley's translation of Elsa Morante's *L'isola di Arturo*. As a guide to the fourth through first millennia B.C., Fernand Braudel, *Memory and the Mediterranean*, edited by Roselyne de Ayala and Paule Braudel, translated by Siân Reynolds (New York: Alfred A. Knopf, 2001), has been impossible to better. My knowledge of Greek religion is owed, in addition to Walter Friedrich Otto, *The Homeric Gods: The Spiritual Significance of Greek Religion*, translated by Moses Hadas (New York: Pantheon, 1954), to W. K. C. Guthrie, *The Greeks and Their Gods* (London: Methuen, 1950);

Paul Veyne, *Did the Greeks Believe in Their Myths? An Essay on the Constitutive Imagination*, translated by Paula Wissing (Chicago: University of Chicago Press, 1988); Walter Burkert, *Greek Religion*, translated by John Raffan (Cambridge, Mass.: Harvard University Press, 1985); and Marcel Detienne and Jean-Pierre Vernant, *Les ruses de l'intelligence* (Paris: Flammarion, 1974). As I've indicated, the English translation of Virgil's *Aeneid* that I quote from is that of Robert Fitzgerald (New York: Random House, 1983). For Auden on Ischia, I have turned to Humphrey Carpenter, *W. H. Auden: A Biography* (London: George Allen & Unwin, 1981), and Thekla Clark, *Wystan and Chester: A Personal Memoir of W. H. Auden and Chester Kallman*, introduction by James Fenton (London: Faber & Faber, 1995). Here and in chapter three, I have quoted from *The Periodic Table* (New York: Schocken Books, 1984), Raymond Rosenthal's translation of Primo Levi's *Il sistema periodico*. The lines from Ariosto's *Orlando furioso* are from the translation by Guido Waldman (Oxford: Oxford University Press, 1983). My source for information on the cholera epidemics is Frank M. Snowden, *Naples in the Time of Cholera, 1884–1911* (Cambridge, England: Cambridge University Press, 1995). The quotation from Sallust is from Roberto Calasso, *The Marriage of Cadmus and Harmony*, translated by Tim Parks (New York: Alfred A. Knopf, 1992).

Two. Four Europes

I have quoted Daniel Mendelsohn's translation of "The Intervention of the Gods" from *C. P. Cavafy: Collected Poems* (New York: Alfred A. Knopf, 2009) and have been instructed by his commentary on the poem. My knowledge of Caesar Augustus is drawn from Arnaldo Momigliano, "Augustus," in *The Oxford Classical Dictionary*, second edition, edited by

N. G. L. Hammond and H. H. Scullard (Oxford: The Clarendon Press, 1970); G. W. Bowersock, *Augustus and the Greek World* (Oxford: Oxford University Press, 1965); and Anthony Everitt, *Augustus: The Life of Rome's First Emperor* (New York: Random House, 2006). What I understand of ancient Roman leisure on the Bay is owed to a man I knew too briefly, John D'Arms, whose *Romans on the Bay of Naples: A Social and Cultural History of the Villas and Their Owners from 150 B.C. to A.D. 400* (Cambridge, Mass.: Harvard University Press, 1970) has lost none of its brilliance after more than forty years. The phrase "style of old age" is from Hermann Broch's introduction to Rachel Bespaloff, *On the Iliad*, translated by Mary McCarthy (New York: Pantheon, 1947). I have also turned to Gottfried Benn's "Artists and Old Age" in *Primal Vision: Selected Writings of Gottfried Benn*, edited by E. B. Ashton (New York: New Directions, 1971), and to Edward W. Said, *On Late Style: Music and Literature Against the Grain*, foreword by Mariam C. Said, introduction by Michael Wood (New York: Pantheon, 2006). As a guide to the religious sea-change of late antiquity, I went to Peter Brown, *The World of Late Antiquity, A.D. 150–750* (Lon-

don: Thames & Hudson, 1971); Richard Fletcher, *The Barbarian Conversion: From Paganism to Christianity* (New York: Marian Wood / Henry Holt, 1998); and Ramsay MacMullen, *Christianity and Paganism in the Fourth to Eighth Centuries* (New Haven: Yale University Press, 1997). A recent, and highly original, view of the triumph of Christianity is Alan Cameron, *The Last Pagans of Rome* (Oxford and New York: Oxford University Press, 2011). The San Gennaro catacombs

Ferragosto in città   are ably described and beautifully illustrated in

Umberto M. Fasola, *Le catacombe di San Gennaro a Capodimonte* (Rome: Editalia, 1975). The translated lines from the *Alcestis* of Euripides are from Richmond Lattimore's version in *Euripides I* (Chicago: University of Chicago Press, 1955). E. H. Gombrich's *A Little History of the World*, translated by Caroline Musthill (New Haven: Yale University Press, 2005), a book intended for young people when the German original appeared in 1936, has helped this adult sort out the Great Migrations of the third through tenth centuries.

Three. The Very True Truths

For the Norman conquest of the South, I have followed John Julius Norwich, *The Normans in the South, 1016–1130* (London: Harlow, Longmans, 1967) and *The Kingdom in the Sun, 1130–1194* (London: Harlow, Longmans, 1970). Georgina Masson's *Frederick II of Hohenstaufen: A Life* (London: Secker & Warburg, 1957) has been essential reading. For Angevin painting, I went to Ferdinando Bologna, *Pittori alla corte angioina, 1266–1414, e un riesame dell'arte nell'età fridericiana* (Rome: U. Bozzi, 1969). For Angevin architecture, I consulted Caroline Bruzelius, *The Stones of Naples: Church Building in Angevin Italy, 1266–1343* (New Haven: Yale University Press, 2004). My understanding of Alfonso the Magnanimous and his Arch is owed to George L. Hersey, *The Aragonese Arch at Naples* (New Haven: Yale University Press, 1973). Hersey's *Alfonso II and the Artistic Renewal of Naples, 1485–1495* (New Haven: Yale University Press, 1969) is my source for the works of Benedetto da Maiano and Guido Mazzoni at Monteoliveto, and for the quotation from Paolo Giovio.

Four. Particulars

The best scholarly book on Michelangelo Merisi remains Howard Hibbard, *Caravaggio* (New York: Harper & Row, 1983). I also consulted Peter Robb's *M: The Man Who Became Caravaggio* (New York: Henry Holt, 2001); Andrew Graham-Dixon's *Caravaggio: A Life Sacred and Profane* (New York: W. W. Norton, 2011); Richard Spear's *From Caravaggio to Artemisia: Essays on Painting in Seventeenth-Century Italy and France* (London: Pindar Press, 2002); and Francine Prose's *Caravaggio: Painter of Miracles* (New York: HarperCollins, 2005). Roger Fry's remarks on Caravaggio are in the commentaries to his edition of Joshua Reynolds's *Discourses Delivered to the Students of the Royal Academy* (London: Seeley, 1905). The quotation from Michael Fried is in his 2002 A. W. Mellon Lectures in the Fine Arts, afterward published as *The Moment of Caravaggio* (Princeton, N.J.: Princeton University Press, 2010). Like all readers of Vico, I am indebted to Isaiah Berlin's *Vico and Herder: Two Studies in the History of Ideas* (New York: Viking, 1976) and Mark Lilla's *G. B. Vico: The Making of an Anti-Modern* (Cambridge, Mass.: Harvard University Press, 1993). Edmund Wilson reflects on Vico in *To the Finland Station: A Study in the Writing and Acting of History* (New York: Harcourt, Brace, 1940). I have quoted from E. H. Gombrich's "André Malraux and the Crisis of Expressionism," in *The Burlington Magazine*, volume 96, number 621 (December 1954). H. V. Morton recalls his journey to Placentia Bay aboard HMS *Prince of Wales* in *Atlantic Meeting* (London: Methuen, 1943.) The best commentary on *That Hamilton Woman* is surely Molly Haskell's accompanying the Criterion Collection DVD of the film. William Hamilton's years at the Neapolitan court are incomparably told by Brian Fothergill in *Sir William Hamilton, Envoy Extraordinary* (New York: Harcourt, Brace & World, 1969). Harold Acton's *The Last*

Bourbons of Naples (1825–1861) (London: Methuen, 1961) has been my source for the brief reign of Francesco II and Maria Sofia. I have also consulted Amedeo Mangone, *Maria Sofia: L'eroina di Gaeta, l'ultima regina di Napoli* (Naples: Grimaldi, 1992), and Arrigo Petacco, *La regina del Sud: Amori e guerre segrete di Maria Sofia di Borbone* (Milan: Mondadori, 1992). Petacco makes his case for Maria Sofia's complicity in the regicide at Monza in *L'anarchico che venne dall'America: Storia di Gaetano Bresci e del complotto per uccidere Umberto I* (Milan: Mondadori, 2000). The quotations from Proust's *La prisonnière* are in D. J. Enright's revision of C. K. Scott Moncrieff and Terence Kilmartin, *In Search of Lost Time* (New York: Modern Library, 1992–1993).

Five. Siren Calls, Siren Echoes

For nonsensational discussions of Tiberius on Capri, I have turned to Thomas Spencer Jerome, "The Tacitean Tiberius: A Study in Historiographic Method," *Classical Philology*, volume 7, number 3 (July 1912; available at http://www.jstor.org/stable/262093), and Edward T. Salmon, *A History of the Roman World from 30 B.C. to A.D. 138* (London: Methuen, 1944). Information about John Ellingham Brooks is by way of Ted Morgan, *Maugham* (New York: Simon & Schuster, 1980), and Selina Hastings, *The Secret Lives of Somerset Maugham* (New York: Random House, 2010). Further items of island gossip are from James Money, *Capri: Island of Pleasure* (London: Hamish Hamilton, 1986). My knowledge of Norman Douglas is owed largely to Mark Holloway, *Norman Douglas: A Biography* (London: Secker & Warburg, 1976). I have quoted from Archibald Colquhoun's translation of Lampedusa's "Lighea" in *The Siren and Selected Writings*, with an introduction by David Gilmour (London:

Scugnizzo, *August 1944*

The Harvill Press, 1995), and from David Richards and Sophie Lund's translation of Bunin's *The Gentleman from San Francisco and Other Stories* (New York: Penguin Books, 1987). The quoted lines from Homer are in Robert Fitzgerald's translation of *The Odyssey* (Garden City, N.Y.: Anchor Press/ Doubleday, 1961). The Oscan inscription beneath Punta della Campanella is documented by Georges Vallet in "La presqu'île de Sorrente dans l'antiquité préromaine: À propos des deux livres récents," which appeared in the *Journal des savants* of the Institut de France, Académie des Inscriptions et de Belles-Lettres, January–June 1993.

Conclusion: Lacrimae Rerum

Albert Camus's lecture "The Human Crisis," which he delivered at Columbia University in 1946, was translated from the French by Lionel Abel and appeared in Dorothy Norman's *Twice a Year* (Fall–Winter, 1946–1947). Aubrey Menin's true-life novel of the September uprising, *The Four Days of Naples* (New York: Seaview Press, 1979), has proved indispensable to my understanding of the Quattro Giornate. For the German destruction of archives deposited at Villa Montesano, I relied on the firsthand narrative by Riccardo Filangieri in his pamphlet *L'Archivio di Stato di Napoli durante la Seconda Guerra Mondiale* (Naples: Arte Tipografica, 1946). My knowledge of the life of Curzio Malaparte comes from Maurizio Serra, *Malaparte: Vies et légendes* (Paris: Bernard Grasset, 2011). I have quoted from *The Skin* (Evanston, Ill.: Northwestern University Press, 1997), David Moore's translation of Malaparte's *La pelle*. For Neapolitan subsistence in the aftermath of the German withdrawal, I turned to Paolo De Marco, *Polvere di piselli: La vita quotidiana durante l'occupazione alleata (1943–1944)* (Naples: Liguori, 1996). John Horne Burns's description of the Allied occupation, *The Gallery* (New York: Harper & Brothers, 1947), is a work of fiction abounding in fact, and invaluable. John Huston, who was in Italy to make U.S. government films, records his memories of Naples under the occupation in *An Open Book* (New York: Alfred A. Knopf, 1980). The passages quoted from Alan Moorehead are in *Eclipse* (New York: Coward-McCann, 1945). The translated lines from Aeschylus's *Prometheus Bound* are from David Grene's version in *Aeschylus II* (Chicago: University of Chicago Press, 1956).

INDEX

Page numbers in italics refer to illustrations. PI refers to the photo insert.

ILLUSTRATION PERMISSIONS

Page 113: Alinari Archives–Alinari Archive, Florence

Page 119: Courtesy Shirley Hazzard

Page 134: Biblioteca Nazionale "Vittorio Emanuele III," Naples, with permission from the Ministero per i Beni e le Attività Culturali–Italia

Page 154: Photograph by Islay Lyons. Walston–Greene Papers, Georgetown University Library Special Collections Research Center, Washington, D.C.

Page 168: Getty Images/FPG

Page 170: © Hulton-Deutsch Collection/Corbis

Page 172: Getty Images/Margaret Bourke-White

Page 178: © Bettmann/Corbis (detail)

Page 187: © Bettmann/Corbis

Page 190: Archivio Carbone

Page 194: © Wayne Miller/Corbis (detail)

Photo insert

Skeleton: © Jonathan Blair/Corbis

Piazza del Plebiscito: Getty Images/Hugo Jaeger

Arcosolium: © Erich Lessing/Art Resource, NY

Pietrasanta bell tower: © Vincenzo Lerro

The Martyrdom of Saint Ursula: Caravaggio (Michelangelo Merisi; Milan, 1571–Porto Ercole, 1610), *Martyrdom of St. Ursula*, 1610. Oil on canvas, 143 x 180 cm. Collezione lntesa Sanpaolo, Palazzo Zevallos Stigliano, Naples

The Seven Acts of Mercy: Michelangelo Merisi da Caravaggio, *Le opere della misericordia* (1607), Chiesa e Quadreria del Pio Monte della Misericordia, Naples. © Archivio dell'Arte/Luciano Pedicini

Majolica cloister: Mimmo Iodice/Corbis

Teatro San Carlo: © Atlantide Phototravel/Corbis

Via Krupp: © John and Lisa Merrill/Corbis

Villa Lysis: © Adalberto Tiburzi

Majolica pavement: Courtesy Benjamin Taylor

Santa Chiara cloister: © Philippe Lissac/Godong/Corbis

Monte Solaro: © Bob Sacha/Corbis

Tattered flyer: © Janet Malcolm